ACCOUNTING DATABASE FUNDAMENTALS

LEARN BY EXAMPLES IN SQL SERVER

Chris Chinaire

Pepukai Press
London, United Kingdom

A CIP catalogue record of this book is available
from the British Library.

Cover design: Saba Art Gallery

ISBN-Print 978-1-9161967-4-2 |E-book 978-1-9161967-5-9
Printed by Ingram Spark

To the memory of my grandmothers:
Ambuya VaHambe and uGogo VaZanka
who taught me the value of hard work
and the importance of family values

*"The writer does the most who gives the reader
the most knowledge
and takes from him the least time"*
–Charles Caleb Colton

Contents

Introduction

The average SQL Developer can decipher the business rules of any system by studying the data model, exploring the transaction processing, and analysing the information retrieval queries and reports. Unfortunately, some have concluded that accounting is the exception after finding it unintuitive.

Many have turned to books on bookkeeping and accounting to study the manual accounting system. And quickly learned that maintaining manual financial records in paper-based accounting books is such a long and tedious process it takes time to be proficient. Preparing and retrieving information from manual financial records is a complex and time-consuming process.

Therefore, some have found it challenging to contribute to the support and customisation of a corporate accounting system or solutions that interface with the accounting module. It is no wonder SQL developers often perceive accounting as complex. This book debunks that notion.

It fast-tracks you from little or no knowledge of accounting to the application of principles. It introduces accounting concepts in simple terms, illustrates how they are applied in a SQL database, and invites you to immediately put into practice what you have learned in line with the timeless wisdom in the famous quote:

> "Tell me, I will forget
> Show me, I will remember
> Let me do, I will understand"
> **Benjamin Franklin**

The objective is to help you understand accounting in the shortest possible time because so many things demand your attention. Your top priority is to stay current with technology trends.

This book incrementally introduces an accounting data model for a sole trader case study. You will gain the most from the book if you follow the ex-

1

amples in your instance of SQL Server. Complexities are omitted to highlight core accounting concepts.

No prior knowledge of accounting is assumed.

CHAPTER 1

Basic concepts

What is accounting?

Accounting is a data management system designed to ingest and process transactions from multiple systems. It maintains structured data stores that facilitate the retrieval of information for internal and statutory reporting purposes.

The diagram below illustrates the inflow of data into the accounting module in the fictitious sole trader, Murewa Consultancy, used in examples throughout the book:

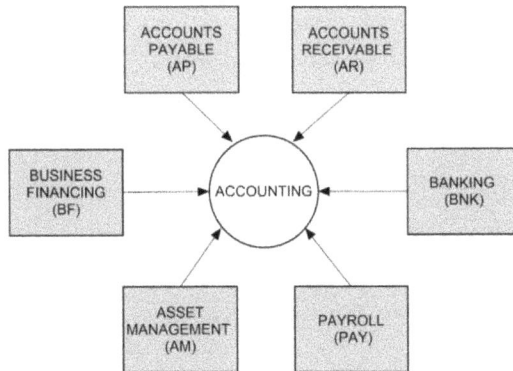

Usage of financial information

Managers use financial information to monitor performance and take necessary measures to improve results. Owners analyse the same information to assess the viability of their investment and decide on a course of action. Employees study the information to evaluate job security and the timing of pay rise negotiations.

Suppliers gauge a business's creditworthiness and ability to pay for goods and services. Lenders' primary interest is the business's ability to repay loans. Tax authorities aim to ensure that businesses are taxed correctly.

Legal structure

This book's examples are based on a sole trader, the simplest legal structure for a business. A sole trader, also known as a sole proprietorship, is a business owned and run by one person.

There is no legal distinction between the owner and the business. Business transactions are kept separate from the owner's personal transactions.

This book illustrates a fictitious sole trader, C Murewa, trading as Murewa Consultancy. The business employs three people and offers IT Consultancy. Monthly expenses include rent for premises, salaries, and utilities.

Type of processes

Three types of processes are covered: transaction, month-end, and year-end.

The transaction process relates to the immediate processing of financial transactions.

The month-end process involves verifying the validity of data processed during the month, closing the financial month, generating financial reports, and preparing for the next month's transaction processing.

The year-end process, which occurs after the month-end process of the last month of the year, includes closing the current year, producing year-end financial reports, and opening the first month of the following year.

Accounting methods

There are two methods of accounting, accrual and cash. The difference between the two is the timing of when revenue and expenses are recognised and recorded.

The cash method accounts for revenue only when money is received and for expenses when money is actually paid out. Therefore, accounting data entry is deferred until cash is received or paid out.

On the other hand, the accrual method accounts for revenue when it is earned and expenses when they are incurred. So, an invoice to a customer and a utility bill are immediately considered revenue and expenses, respectively.

The accrual method serves as the basis for the examples in this book.

Purpose of the sample database

A sample database, SOKO, processes transactions and stores accounting data. The data model, which is incrementally introduced, is designed with the following goals in mind:

a) Minimise the ambiguity of the application of accounting principles
b) Enable consistent processing of financial transactions
c) Support verification of data from summary to transactional detail
d) Facilitate efficient information retrieval to produce financial statements
e) Allow retrospective production of financial statements

Figure 1.2, below, shows the symbols used to portray the relationships between tables:

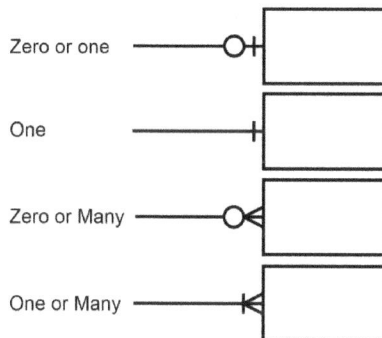

Zero or one

One

Zero or Many

One or Many

CHAPTER 2

The foundation

Cornerstone

A simple equation is the cornerstone of accounting. On the left side are the resources owned by a business, and on the other side are the resources that financed them.

Resources owned by a business are called assets. Finance by the owner is referred to as owner's equity, and borrowed resources (loans) are liabilities. This can be illustrated by the following relationship known as the accounting equation:

$$\text{assets} = \text{liabilities} + \text{owner's equity}$$

An increase in either liabilities or owner's equity results in an equal rise in assets. Similarly, a decrease in assets triggers an equal reduction in either liabilities or owner's equity.

Assets, liabilities, and owner's equity are called permanent accounts because their balances are carried forward from one accounting year to the next.

Income generated is called revenue. It increases both assets and equity. Costs incurred in generating revenue and operating the business are referred to as expenses. They decrease both assets and equity. Resources taken from the business by the owner for personal use are called withdrawals and decrease assets and equity.

The effects of revenue, expenses, and withdrawals are applied to assets and liabilities immediately after a transaction occurs. The impact on equity is deferred to the end of the financial year. During the financial year, the financial position of the business is expressed by the following expanded accounting equation:

assets = liabilities + owner's equity + revenue – expenses - withdrawals

Balances of revenue, expenses, and withdrawals are temporarily accumulated, applied to equity at year-end, and initialised to start the next financial year from zero. Therefore, revenue, expenses, and withdrawals are considered part of the owner's equity and are referred to as temporary or nominal accounts.

The algebra addition rule rewrites the expression as:

assets + expenses + withdrawals = liabilities + owner's equity + revenue

The left side is called debit, and the right side, credit.

A static SQL table, ACCOUNTING_EQUATION, described below, is the centrepiece of the SOKO database:

Column Name	Description	Type	Length	Null	Key	Foreign Table
ELEMENT_ID	Unique identifier	int		N	P	
ELEMENT	Name of Element	varchar	20	N		
SIDE	Side of Accounting Equation	varchar	6	N		
ELEMENT_TYPE	Permanent or Temporary	varchar	10	N		

Each row in the listing below represents an element of the accounting equation and the highest level at which accounting data is summarised:

ELEMENT_KEY	ELEMENT	SIDE	ACCOUNT_TYPE
1	Assets	Debit	Permanent
2	Liabilities	Credit	Permanent
3	Owner's Equity	Credit	Permanent
4	Revenue	Credit	Temporary
5	Expenses	Debit	Temporary
6	Withdrawals	Debit	Temporary

Accounts

The term account has several meanings in accounting. Elements of the accounting equation are often referred to as accounts.

The set of financial reports produced at the end of the year is called the final accounts. One of the reports produced is a profit and loss account, also known as an income statement.

In this context, an account is the level at which the effects of transactions are recorded. It is the lowest level at which business transactions are tracked. Typical accounts include computer hardware, office furniture, rent, bank account, and wages.

The choice of accounts depends on the types of transactions anticipated and the level of detail required for reporting. For one business, an office equipment account may be adequate, while separate accounts for photocopiers and computer hardware best serve the reporting needs of another.

Murewa Consultancy tracks financial activities in the business using the following accounts (grouped by accounting equation element):

Assets

Account	What is tracked
Checking account	Deposits, payments, charges, and transfers
Savings account	Deposits, transfers and interest earnings
Accounts receivable	Amounts owed by customers
Office furniture	Office furniture bought for use in the business
Computer hardware	Computer hardware bought for productive use
Vehicles	Vehicles bought for business use
Land and property	Land and property acquired

Liabilities

Account	What is tracked
Accounts payable	Amounts owed to suppliers of services
Income Tax Payable	Income tax payable
Net Pay	Net pay due to employees
Long-term loan	Long-term loan taken
Mortgage Loan	Mortgage loan taken

Owner's Equity

Account	What is tracked
Capital	Direct investment by the owner

Revenue

Account	What is tracked
Consultancy Revenue	Consultancy revenue generated
Interest earned	Savings account interest earnings

Expenses

Account	What is tracked
Office rent	Office rent expense
Staff salaries	Staff salaries
Utilities	Gas, electricity, and water billings
Travel	Business travel expenses
Office sundries	Office sundries expenses
Loan Interest	Interest on loan charged by the lender
Bank charges	Checking account bank charges

Withdrawals

Account	What is tracked
Drawings	Drawings of funds or assets by the owner for personal use

The diagram below portrays the relationship between the ACCOUNTS and the ACCOUNTING_EQUATION tables:

The structure of the ACCOUNT table is finalised in the next chapter.

CHAPTER 3

Building blocks to support reporting

Starting with the end in mind

The earlier we consider what needs to be in place to enable information retrieval, the easier the task will be when we explore reporting. Therefore, the content and structure of each financial statement are analysed to determine the SQL tables required and their corresponding structures.

Income Statement

The Income Statement (Profit and Loss Statement) is a standard report that uses revenue and expenses elements to calculate the Net Income (Profit or Loss), as shown in the sample below:

Murewa Consultancy Income Statement for month ending December 31, 2022	
Revenues	
Consultancy Revenue	0.00
Interest earned	0.00
Total Revenues	0.00
Expenses	
Office rent	0.00
Staff Salaries	0.00
Utilities	0.00
Travel	0.00
Office sundries	0.00
Loan Interest	0.00
Bank Charges	0.00
Total Expenses	0.00
Net Income (Profit/Loss)	0.00

Types of revenue are listed and summed up, followed by types of expenses, which are also aggregated. The difference between the two is Net Income, which can be either a profit or a loss.

Report headers and labels are held in the ACCOUNTING_EQUATION and ACCOUNT tables.

Balance Sheet Statement

What is immediately apparent in the sample Balance Sheet Statement below?

Murewa Consultancy Balance Sheet as at 31 December 2022			
ASSETS		**LIABILITIES & EQUITY**	
		Liabilities	
Current Assets		Current Liabilities	
Checking account	0.00	Accounts payable	0.00
Savings account	0.00	Income Tax payable	0.00
Accounts receivable	0.00	**Total Current Liabilities**	**0.00**
Total Current Assets	**0.00**		
		Long-term Liabilities	
Long-term Assets		Bank Loan	0.00
Office furniture	0.00	Mortgage Loan	0.00
Computer hardware	0.00	**Long-term Liabilities**	**0.00**
Land	0.00		
Total Long-term Assets	**0.00**	Owner's Equity	
		Capital	0.00
		Net Income (Revenue - Expenses)	0.00
		Less Withdrawals	0.00
			0.00
Total Assets	**0.00**	**Total Liabilities and Owner's Equity**	**0.00**

Do you notice that the report is a more detailed version of the accounting equation? This is why the accounting equation is also referred to as the balance sheet equation. The above is a horizontal balance sheet displaying both sides of the accounting equation. The following chapters show that the same information can also be presented in a vertical format.

The sample Balance Sheet report shows that each permanent element is broken down into categories used by every organisation. The following universal definition of each category ensures consistency and comparability of financial reporting across different organisations.

Assets

- Current assets

  Current assets are immediately available to meet a business's short-term obligations. These assets are convertible to cash within a year and include cash, cash equivalents, accounts receivable (amounts owed by customers), and stock inventory.

- Long-term assets

  Long-term assets are acquired for their productive use and are not expected to be sold or converted to cash within a year. Examples include office furniture, vehicles, office buildings, and land.

Liabilities

- Current liabilities

  Current liabilities are short-term financial obligations that are due within one year. They include accounts payable (monies owed for goods or services), short-term debt, and income taxes due.

- Long-term liabilities

  Long-term financial obligations that are not expected to be settled within a year are referred to as long-term liabilities. Examples include long-term loans and mortgage loans.

Owner's Equity

- Capital

  Capital represents the resources invested in the business by the owner. The resources may be cash or another type of asset, such as a vehicle.

- Net Income (Profit/Loss)

  The difference between Revenue and Expenses is Net income, which can be either profit or loss.

- Drawings

  Drawings are the owner's withdrawal of funds or assets from the business for personal use.

The SOKO database stores the balance sheet categories in the SQL table BS_CATEGORY, described below:

Column Name	Description	Type	Length	Null	Key	Foreign Table
CATEGORY_ID	Unique identifier	int		N	P	
ELEMENT_ID	Element Identifier	Int		N	F	ACCOUNTING_EQUATION
CATEGORY	Balance Sheet Category	varchar	40	N		

The BS_CATEGORY table listing below depicts the structure and order of the balance sheet equation (accounting equation):

CATEGORY_ID	ELEMENT_KEY	CATEGORY
1	1	Current Assets
2	1	Long-term Assets
3	2	Current Liabilities
4	2	Long-term Liabilities
5	3	Capital
6	3	Net Income (Profit/Loss)
7	3	Drawings

The table has a many-to-one relationship with the ACCOUNTING_EQUATION table as shown below:

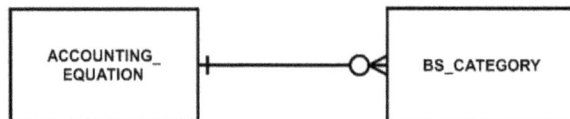

Cash Flow Statement

What can you glean from the bare-bones Cash Flow Statement below?

Murewa Consultancy Statement of Cash Flows for year ending December 31, 2022	
Cash flows from Operating activities	0.00
Cash flows from Investing activities	0.00
Cash flows from Financing activities	0.00
Net increase (decrease) in cash	**0.00**
Cash at the beginning of the year	0.00
Cash at the end of the year	**0.00**

The report monitors the inflows and outflows of cash and cash equivalents (CCE) in the business. CCEs are cash on hand and current assets immediately convertible to cash, such as demand deposits, checking accounts, and highly liquid investments.

The report helps ensure the business meets short-term obligations (current liabilities). Incoming and outgoing cash is grouped into the following activities:

- *Operating activities* are the daily activities a business does to produce and sell its services or products, as well as expenses it incurs in running and maintaining the business.
- *Investing activities* are cash transactions associated with buying long-term assets for use in the business and their disposal at the end of their useful lives.
- *Finance activities* are cash transactions that involve long-term liabilities and owner's equity.

There are two methods for presenting cash flow: the direct and indirect methods. The direct method presents actual cash flows, whereas the indirect method involves calculations based on changes to accounts payable and receivable, as well as other adjustments.

Although national and international accounting standard-setting bodies recommend the direct method, most organisations use the indirect method because it is perceived as easier and less time-consuming.

The SOKO database uses the direct method. Activities are held in the SQL table ACTIVITY, which is described below:

Column Name	Description	Type	Length	Null	Key	Foreign Table
ACTIVITY_ID	Unique identifier	int		N	P	
ACTIVITY	Cash flow activity	varchar	20	N		

The table below lists the activities in the order they appear in the Cash Flow Statement:

ACTIVITY KEY	ACTIVITY
1	Operating
2	Investing
3	Finance

The more detailed version of the Cash Flow Statement below shows the sources of cash and how it was spent:

Murewa Consultancy Statement of Cash Flows for year ending December 31, 2022	
Operating Activities	
Cash received from customers	0.00
Interest Received	0.00
Cash paid to Employees	0.00
Cash paid for Income Tax	0.00
Cash paid for other operating expenses	0.00
Net cash from Operating Activities [A]	**0.00**
Investing Activities	
Purchase of property and equipment	0.00
Sale of property and equipment	0.00
Net cash from Investing Activities [B]	**0.00**
Financing Activities	
Add: Investment by the owner	0.00
Add: long-term debt	0.00
Less: Repayments of long-term debt	0.00
Less: Withdrawals by the owner	0.00
Net cash from Financing Activities [C]	**0.00**
Net Increase (Decrease) in Cash and Cash Equivalents (A+B+C)	**0.00**
Beginning Cash Balance	**0.00**
Ending Cash Balance	**0.00**

Categories for each activity are stored in the SQL table CF_CATEGORY, described below:

Column Name	Description	Type	Length	Null	Key	Foreign Table
CF_ID	Unique identifier	int		N	P	
ACTIVITY_ID	Activity identifier	Int		N	F	ACTIVITY
CATEGORY	Category description	varchar	50	N		

The table rows below are sorted by activity and category:

CF_ID	ACTIVITY_ID	CATEGORY
1	1	Cash received from customers
2	1	Interest received
3	1	Cash paid to Employees
4	1	Cash paid for Income Tax
5	1	Cash paid for other operating expenses
6	2	Purchase of property and equipment
7	2	Sale of property and equipment
8	3	Add: Investment by the owner
9	3	Add: long-term debt
10	3	Less: Repayments of long-term debt
11	3	Less: Withdrawals by the owner

Account table structure

Now that data retrieval and reporting requirements have been clarified, the structure of the ACCOUNT table can be finalised. The table has a many-to-one relationship with the ACCOUNTING_EQUATION and BS_CATEGORY tables, as shown below:

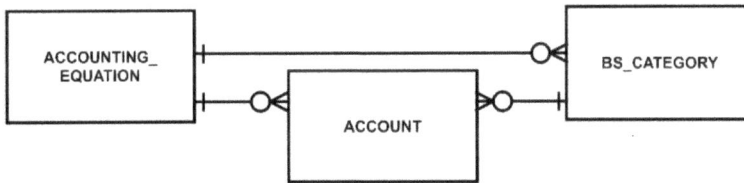

The ACCOUNT table structure is listed below:

Column Name	Description	Type	Length	Null	Key	Foreign Table
ACCT_KEY	Unique identifier	int		N	P	
ELEMENT_ID	Element Id	int		N	F	ACCOUNTING _EQUATION
CATEGORY_ID	Balance Sheet Category Id	int		N	F	BS_CATEGORY
ACCT_ID	Account code	int		N		
ACCT_NAME	Account name	varchar	40	N		
CCE_INT	1-Cash Equivalents; 0-Other	bit		N		
STATUS_IND	0 – Active; 1 – Inactive	bit		N		

Chart of Accounts

A chart of accounts is a complete list of accounts used in an organisation. The SOKO database uses the following 23 accounts, grouped by element of the accounting equation.

Assets

ACCT_KEY	ELEMENT_ID	CATEGORY_ID	ACCT_ID	ACCT_NAME	CCE_IND	STATUS_IND
1	1	1	1000	Checking account	1	0
2	1	1	1010	Savings account	1	0
3	1	1	1020	Accounts receivable	0	0
4	1	2	1500	Office furniture	0	0
5	1	2	1510	Computer hardware	0	0
6	1	2	1520	Vehicles	0	0
7	1	2	1530	Land and property	0	0

Liabilities

ACCT_KEY	ELEMENT_ID	CATEGORY_ID	ACCT_ID	ACCT_NAME	CCE_IND	STATUS_IND
8	2	3	2000	Accounts payable	0	0
9	2	3	2010	Income Tax Payable	0	0
10	2	3	2020	Net Pay	0	0
11	2	4	2500	Long-term loan	0	0
12	2	4	2510	Mortgage loan	0	0

Owner's Equity

ACCT_KEY	ELEMENT_ID	CATEGORY_ID	ACCT_ID	ACCT_NAME	CCE_IND	STATUS_IND
13	3	5	3000	Capital	0	0

Revenue

ACCT_KEY	ELEMENT_ID	CATEGORY_ID	ACCT_ID	ACCT_NAME	CCE_IND	STATUS_IND
14	4	6	4000	Consultancy	0	0
15	4	6	4010	Interest	0	0

Expenses

ACCT_KEY	ELEMENT_ID	CATEGORY_ID	ACCT_ID	ACCT_NAME	CCE_IND	STATUS_IND
16	5	6	5000	Office rent	0	0
17	5	6	5010	Staff salaries	0	0
18	5	6	5020	Utilities	0	0
19	5	6	5030	Travel	0	0
20	5	6	5035	Office sundries	0	0
21	5	6	5040	Loan Interest	0	0
22	5	6	5050	Bank Charges	0	0

Drawings

ACCT_KEY	ELEMENT_ID	CATEGORY_ID	ACCT_ID	ACCT_NAME	CCE_IND	STATUS_IND
23	6	7	6000	Drawings	0	0

The accounts cater for the types of transactions anticipated and the level of reporting detail required. The chart of accounts is not set in stone. It is expected to evolve to keep pace with changing business needs.

The table can have new rows, and the ACCT_ID column sorts the accounts in the required order.

The column CCE_IND (Cash or Cash Equivalent Indicator) marks cash and cash equivalent accounts.

Once inserted, an account row is not deleted from the table. The STATUS_IND column is set to 1, indicating that it is inactive.

The accounts cater for the types of transactions anticipated and the level of reporting detail required. The chart of accounts is not set in stone. It is expected to evolve to keep pace with changing business needs.

The table can have new rows, and the ACCT_ID column sorts the accounts in the required order.

CHAPTER 4

Financial data stores

Accounting period and month

F inancial data is processed and stored in the context of months and years. It is logical to start by exploring these periods.

A financial year, or an accounting period, is the twelve consecutive months a business records, collates, and reports its annual financial information.

The financial year does not always coincide with the calendar year. Similarly, a financial month may be based on the calendar or specific data ranges, such as March 15 to April 14, April 15 to May 14, etc.

SOKO database holds financial years in the FISCAL_YEAR table and months in the FISCAL_MONTH table. The figure below shows the relationship between the two tables:

FISCAL_YEAR table

The structure of the FISCAL_YEAR table is as follows:

Column Name	Description	Type	Length	Null	Key	Foreign Table
YEAR_ID	Unique identifier	Int		N	P	
START_DATE	Start of Fiscal Year	Date		N		
END_DATE	End of Fiscal Year	Date	40	N		
COMMENTS	Comments (if any)	varchar	30	Y		
YEAR_STATUS	BLANK, OPEN, CLOSED	varchar	6	Y		

The listing below shows the current year with an OPEN status, including the start and end dates, as well as details for the following year:

YEAR_ID	START_DATE	END_DATE	COMMENTS	YEAR_STATUS
2024	01/04/2023	31/03/2024		OPEN
2025	01/04/2024	31/03/2025		

FISCAL_MONTH table

The FISCAL_MONTH table is structured as follows:

Column Name	Description	Type	Length	Null	Key	Foreign Table
MNTH _ID	Unique Identifier	int		N	P	
YEAR_ID	Year Id	int		N	F	FISCAL_YEAR
START_DATE	Month Start Date	date		Y		
END_DATE	End of the month date	date		Y		
COMMENTS	Comments (if any)	varchar	30	Y		
MONTH_STATUS	BLANK, OPEN, CLOSED	varchar	6	Y		

The listing below shows the monthly details for the fiscal year 2024:

MNTH_ID	YEAR_ID	START_DATE	END_DATE	COMMENTS	MONTH_STATUS
202400	2024			2024 Opening Balances	
202401	2024	01/04/2023	30/04/2023		OPEN
202402	2024	01/05/2023	31/05/2023		
202403	2024	01/06/2023	30/06/2023		
202404	2024	01/07/2023	31/07/2023		
202405	2024	01/08/2023	31/08/2023		
202406	2024	01/09/2023	30/09/2023		
202407	2024	01/10/2023	31/10/2023		
202408	2024	01/11/2023	30/11/2023		
202409	2024	01/12/2023	31/12/2023		
202410	2024	01/01/2024	31/01/2024		
202411	2024	01/02/2024	29/02/2024		
202412	2024	01/03/2024	31/03/2024		
202413	2024			Closing Temp Accounts	

It is understandable to expect 12 months in a year. The two extra months, 00 and 13, are added for functional purposes. Month 00 is used to record opening balances for the year, and Month 13 is used to transfer balances of temporary accounts to a permanent account, e.g., the Capital account.

Financial data tables

The SOKO database holds financial data in two tables, JOURNAL and LEDGER. The JOURNAL table keeps records of the dual effects of every transaction, which are either an increase or a decrease in the balance of each affected account.

The LEDGER is a monthly summary of journal entries for every account. The table holds each month's effective changes to the balance of every account.

Both tables have a many-to-one relationship with the ACCOUNT and FISCAL_MONTH tables, as shown below:

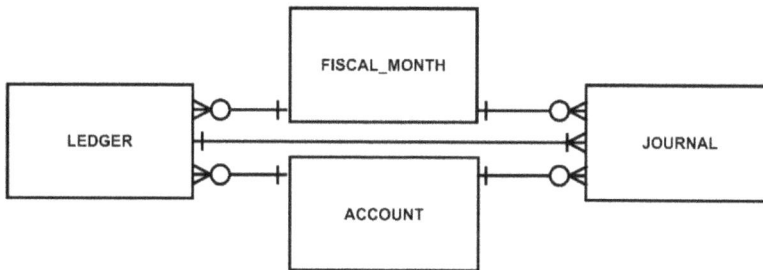

The financial data in the tables is based on the foundations of the accounting equation. The JOURNAL table, or equivalent, in every accounting system worldwide has the following four sets of dual entries:

SET	EFFECT	
	DEBIT SIDE	CREDIT SIDE
1	Increase	Increase
2	Decrease	Decrease
3	Increase and Decrease	
4		Increase and Decrease

Both tables have columns labelled DEBIT and CREDIT that hold changes (increases or decreases) to the balance of each affected account.

The term "debit" or "credit" indicates either an increase or decrease, depending on the account's side of the equation.

The rules are held in the SQL table JRNL_ENTRY_RULES, described below:

Column Name	Description	Type	Length	Null	Key	Foreign Table
JE_RULE_KEY	Unique Identifier	Int		N	P	
SIDE	Accounting Equation Side	varchar	6	N		
EFFECT	Increase or Decrease	varchar	8	N		
JE_TYPE	Type of Journal	varchar	6	N		

The table rules, driven by the account's side of the equation and the effect of the transaction, are listed below:

JE_RULE_KEY	SIDE	EFFECT	JE_TYPE
1	DEBIT	Increase	Debit
2	CREDIT	Increase	Credit
3	DEBIT	Decrease	Credit
4	CREDIT	Decrease	Debit

Journal entries illustration

Journal Entry Steps

1. Identify the accounts affected by a transaction and the effect on each account, either an increase or a decrease to the balance.
2. Determine each account's side of the equation.
3. Apply the rules held in the SQL table, JRNL_ENTRY_RULES.
4. For each account affected, record/enter the following details:

Transaction Date

Account

Transaction Reference

Fiscal month

Narrative (Description of transaction)

Debit

Credit

Examples

How about a walk-through from transaction to journal entries using a real-world example?

C Murewa, who started trading on April 12, 2023, had five pre-analysed transactions in April 2023.

TRANSACTION	REF	DATE	MNTH_ID	AMOUNT	ACCOUNT	EFFECT
Trans A	101	Apr 12 2023	202401	£100.00	Acct 1	Increase
					Acct 2	Increase
Trans B	734	Apr 14 2023	202401	£50.00	Acct 4	Increase
					Acct 1	Decrease
Trans C	A342	Apr 28 2023	202401	£30.00	Acct 3	Increase
					Acct 2	Decrease
Trans D	B901	Apr 30 2023	202401	£10.00	Acct 1	Decrease
					Acct 3	Decrease
Trans E	X908	Apr 31 2023	202401	£5.00	Acct 1	Decrease
					Acct 4	Increase

The four accounts affected, two on each side of the accounting equation, are as follows:

ACCOUNT	SIDE
Acct 1	DEBIT
Acct 2	CREDIT
Acct 3	CREDIT
Acct 4	DEBIT

Task: Create the following table (with 10 rows) in your preferred spreadsheet or word processor and record the journal entries for the above transactions:

TRAN_DATE	REF	ACCOUNT	MNTH_ID	NARRATION	DEBIT	CREDIT

Remember to apply the rules in step 3.

Answer: How do your journal entries compare to the following?

TRAN_DATE	REF	ACCOUNT	MNTH_ID	NARRATIVE	DEBIT	CREDIT
2023-01-12	101	Acct 1	202401	Trans A	100.00	
2023-01-12	101	Acct 2	202401	Trans A		100.00
2023-01-14	734	Acct 4	202401	Trans B	50.00	
2023-01-14	734	Acct 1	202401	Trans B		50.00
2023-01-28	A342	Acct 3	202401	Trans C		30.00
2023-01-28	A342	Acct 2	202401	Trans C	30.00	
2023-01-30	B901	Acct 1	202401	Trans D		10.00
2023-01-30	B901	Acct 3	202401	Trans D	10.00	
2023-01-31	X908	Acct 1	202401	Trans E	5.00	
2023-01-31	X908	Acct 4	202401	Trans E		5.00

Create separate tables for each account, like the one for Acct 1 journal entries below:

TRAN_DATE	REF	ACCOUNT	MNTH_ID	NARRATIVE	DEBIT	CREDIT
2023-01-12	101	Acct 1	202401	Trans A	100.00	
2023-01-14	734	Acct 1	202401	Trans B		50.00
2023-01-30	B901	Acct 1	202401	Trans D		10.00
2023-01-31	X908	Acct 1	202401	Trans E	5.00	

Effective movement of each account

The difference between total debits and total credits is the effective movement of each account in a month.

If the total debit is a higher amount, the account has a debit movement; otherwise, it has a credit movement, as illustrated below:

Acct 1

	DEBIT	CREDIT
Totals	105.00	60.00
Effective Movement	45.00	

Acct 2

	DEBIT	CREDIT
Totals	30.00	100.00
Effective Movement		70.00

Acct 3

	DEBIT	CREDIT
Totals	10.00	30.00
Effective Movement		20.00

Acct 4

	DEBIT	CREDIT
Totals	50.00	5.00
Effective Movement	45.00	

Equality check

Balances of all the accounts must be in sync with the accounting equation. So, based on each account's side of the equation, the following expression must be true:

$$Acct\ 1 + Acct\ 4 = Acct\ 2 + Acct\ 3$$

JOURNAL table structure

The following is the JOURNAL table structure in the SOKO database:

Column Name	Description	Type	Length	Null	Key	Foreign Table
ROW_NUM	Unique identifier	bigint		N	P	
JRNL_NUM	Journal number	int		N	F	TRANS
ACCT_KEY	Account Key	int		N	F	ACCOUNT
TRAN_DATE	Transaction Date	date		N		
TRAN_REF	Transaction	varchar	30	N		
MNTH_ID	Fiscal month	int		N	F	FISCAL_MONTH
NARRATIVE	Transaction narrative	varchar	60	N		
DEBIT	Amount debited	money		Y		
CREDIT	Amount Credited	money		Y		
CF_ID	Cash Flow	int		Y	F	CF_CATEGORY

The table is designed to optionally capture the cash flow category for transactions that affect any cash or cash equivalent account.

Posting to the Ledger

Posting is the process of moving journal entries to the LEDGER. Journal entries may be accumulated over hours for processing at specific times. So, in between postings, the JOURNAL and LEDGER tables are out of sync.

The other option is to post at the same time as the journal entry. It ensures that the JOURNAL and LEDGER tables are always in sync. Our sample database is designed to post immediately after a journal entry is made. Therefore, every journal entry updates the monthly movements for each account in the ledger.

The ten journal entries that we have looked at so far update the LEDGER as follows:

ACCOUNT	MNTH_ID	DEBIT	CREDIT
Acct 1	202401	45.00	
Acct 2	202401		70.00
Acct 3	202401		20.00
Acct 4	202401	45.00	

An account typically has one entry per fiscal month. The structure of the LEDGER table in the SOKO database is as follows:

Column Name	Description	Type	Length	Null	Key	Foreign Table
ROW_NUM	Unique identifier	bigint		N	P	
ACCT_KEY	Account Key	int		N	F	ACCOUNT
MNTH_ID	Fiscal month ID	int		N	F	FISCAL_MONTH
DEBIT	Amount debited (if any)	money		Y		
CREDIT	Amount Credited (if any)	money		Y		

The table has three types of rows: monthly movements (which we have just explored), opening balances for the year, and year-end clearing of temporary accounts.

Balances

The balance of an account is calculated from every increase and decrease (debit or credit) since the business started. Having opening balances for each financial year simplifies the calculation.

The difference between the total debits and credits in a fiscal year, starting from the opening balances of the year, is the balance of each account at a selected period.

Accounts on the debit (left-hand) side have a debit balance (Debit — Credit), and accounts on the other side have a credit balance (Credit — Debit). The balances are used in preparing financial statements.

CHAPTER 5

Preparing for transactions

You have so far learned that transactions are the source of accounting data. How the data lands in accounting varies from organisation to organisation.

Some small businesses pass paper documents, such as invoices, receipts, bills, and bank statements, to their bookkeepers or accountants. Others capture the data in pre-formatted spreadsheets, which are periodically sent via email.

Some use online commercial accounting packages to enter data and remotely collaborate with accountants.

Large firms, with millions of daily transactions generated across separate business units in different countries, automate the data flow into accounting.

This book simulates data feeds from six modules used by the fictitious trader, Murewa Consultancy, into accounting.

Every transaction from each module is recorded in the TRANS table and used to update the JOURNAL and the LEDGER. The same data is held in the three forms illustrated below:

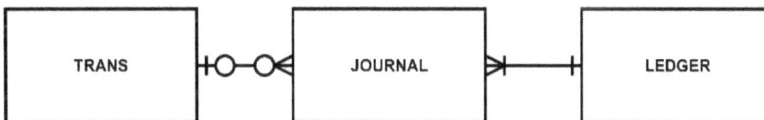

Types of transactions

To automate the processing of incoming data, it is essential to know three things in advance: the source module, the type of transaction, and the expected data columns.

The SQL table, TRAN_TYPE, described below, holds the details of every type of transaction anticipated:

Column Name	Description	Type	Length	Null	Key	Foreign Table
TRAN_TYPE_ID	Unique identifier	int		N	P	
MODULE	Module abbreviation	varchar	3	N		
TRAN_TYPE	Transaction type description	varchar	50	N		
COLUMNS	Comma delimited columns	varchar	80	N		

Every type of transaction anticipated from each module is loaded into the table, with sufficient detail provided to enable processing.

Business Financing (BF)

The Business Financing module manages the flow of funds between the business and its owner, as well as between the business and lenders. The module's six types of data feeds are recorded in the TRAN_TYPE table as follows:

TRAN_TYPE_ID	MODULE	TRAN_TYPE	COLUMNS
1	BF	Owner cash contribution	TRAN_DATE,REF_ID,AMOUNT
2	BF	Owner cash withdrawal	TRAN_DATE,REF_ID,AMOUNT
3	BF	Long-term business loan	TRAN_DATE,REF_ID,AMOUNT
4	BF	Long-term loan payment	TRAN_DATE,REF_ID,AMOUNT, INTEREST,PRINCIPAL
5	BF	Mortgage loan	TRAN_DATE,REF_ID,AMOUNT
6	BF	Mortgage loan payment	TRAN_DATE,REF_ID,AMOUNT, INTEREST,PRINCIPAL

Asset Management (AM)

The asset management module manages the lifecycle of all long-term assets within the business, including computer hardware, office furniture, and vehicles.

It keeps up-to-date records of procurement (by bank card), usage, and disposal of assets and has the following initial data feeds to accounting:

TRAN_TYPE_ID	MODULE	TRAN_TYPE	COLUMNS
7	AM	Computer hardware purchase	TRAN_DATE,REF_ID,AMOUNT
8	AM	Office furniture purchase	TRAN_DATE,REF_ID,AMOUNT
9	AM	Vehicle purchase	TRAN_DATE,REF_ID,AMOUNT

Accounts payable (AP)

The accounts payable module records vendors (suppliers of goods and services), vendor bills, and payments made to vendors. It generates the following data feeds to accounting:

TRAN_TYPE_ID	MODULE	TRAN_TYPE	COLUMNS
10	AP	Utility bill	TRAN_DATE,REF_ID,AMOUNT
11	AP	Utility bill payment	TRAN_DATE,REF_ID,AMOUNT
12	AP	Office rent payment	TRAN_DATE,REF_ID,AMOUNT
13	AP	Travel/Fuel payment	TRAN_DATE,REF_ID,AMOUNT
14	AP	Office sundries payment	TRAN_DATE,REF_ID,AMOUNT

Accounts receivable (AR)

The accounts receivable module manages customers, generates customer invoices, records cash receipts, and tracks outstanding receivables. The following data feeds are generated for accounting:

TRAN_TYPE_ID	MODULE	TRAN_TYPE	COLUMNS
15	AR	Customer invoice	TRAN_DATE,REF_ID,AMOUNT
16	AR	Client cash receipt	TRAN_DATE,REF_ID,AMOUNT

Payroll (PAY)

The simplified monthly payroll system calculates salaries, aggregates gross pay, determines income tax payable, and calculates the total net pay. It maintains records of income tax payments and total net salary payments.

The data feeds to accounting are added to the TRAN_TYPE table as follows:

TRAN_TYPE_ID	MODULE	TRAN_TYPE	COLUMNS
17	PAY	Monthly payroll	TRAN_DATE,REF_ID,AMOUNT, INCOME_TAX,NET_PAY
18	PAY	Income tax payment	TRAN_DATE, REF_ID,AMOUNT
19	PAY	Net salary payment	TRAN_DATE, REF_ID,AMOUNT

Banking (BNK)

Online banking manages the checking and savings accounts, tracks inter-account transfers, and downloads bank charges, interest earned, and transfers to and from each account.

The following data feeds to accounting are added to the TRAN_TYPE table:

TRAN_TYPE_ID	MODULE	TRAN_TYPE	COLUMNS
20	BNK	Transfer to Savings Account	TRAN_DATE,REF_ID,AMOUNT
21	BNK	Transfer to Checking Account	TRAN_DATE,REF_ID,AMOUNT
22	BNK	Bank charges payment	TRAN_DATE,REF_ID,AMOUNT
23	BNK	Interest earned	TRAN_DATE,REF_ID,AMOUNT

Transaction table structure

The structure of the TRANS table, described below, accommodates every column in every anticipated type of transaction.

Column Name	Description	Type	Length	Null	Key	Foreign Table
TRAN_DATE	Date of transaction	date		N		
TRAN_TYPE_ID	Type of transaction	int		N	F	TRAN_TYPE
REF_ID	Source module reference	varchar	15	N		
AMOUNT	Amount value	money		N		
INTEREST	Interest value	money		Y		
PRINCIPAL	Principal value	money		Y		
INCOME_TAX	Income tax deducted	money		Y		
NET_SALARY	Net salary	money		Y		
JRNL_NUM	Journal Num (auto generated)	bigint		N		

The monetary columns INTEREST, PRINCIPAL, INCOME_TAX, and NET_SALARY are nullable and conditionally populated depending on the type of transaction.

Effects of each type of transaction

To automate transaction processing, it is essential to analyse and store the following details (for each type of transaction anticipated):

- Every account affected
- Effect on each account (increase or decrease)
- Type of journal entry to be generated for each account (depending on the account's side of the equation and the effect)
- The amount column (in the TRANS table)
- Cash flow category (if applicable)

The SQL table TRAN_TYPE_EFFECT, described below, is structured to store the effects of every anticipated transaction type:

Column Name	Description	Type	Length	Null	Key	Foreign Table
ROW_NUM	Unique Id	int		N	P	
TRAN_TYPE_ID	Type of transaction	int		N	F	TRAN_TYPE
ACCT_KEY	Account key	Int		N	F	ACCOUNT
EFFECT	Increase or Decrease	varchar	8	N		
JRNL_ TYPE	DEBIT or CREDIT	varchar	6	N		
AMOUNT_COLUMN	Amount value column	varchar	20	N		
CF_ID	Cash flow category ID	int		Y	F	CF_CATEGORY

As illustrated in the last chapter, the side of the equation of the account affected and the effect (increase or decrease) determine the journal entry type.

Once populated, the TRAN_TYPE_EFFECT table drives the generation of journal entries and updates of the ledger. The table must be correctly populated.

The relationship between the three tables, TRANS, TRAN_TYPE, and TRAN_TYPE_EFFECT, is illustrated below:

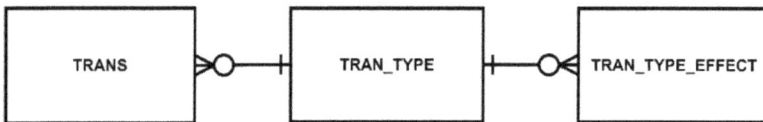

Analysis of types of transactions

Each module's types of transaction are analysed, and the effects are stored, as shown below:

Business Financing (BF)

- Owner cash contribution

  Owner cash contribution increases the Capital account (Credit side) and Checking account (Debit side) by the AMOUNT column value. Cash flow movement is categorised as 'Add: Investment by the owner'. The effects are recorded in the TRAN_TYPE_EFFECT table as:

ROW_NUM	TRAN_TYPE_ID	ACCT_KEY	EFFECT	JRNL_TYPE	AMOUNT_COLUMN	CF_ID
1	1	13	INCREASE	CREDIT	AMOUNT	
2	1	1	INCREASE	DEBIT	AMOUNT	8

- Owner cash withdrawal

  Owner cash withdrawal increases the Drawings account (Debit side) and decreases the Checking account (Debit side) by the AMOUNT column value. The cash flow is categorised as 'Less: Withdrawals by the owner'. The following two rows are added to the TRAN_TYPE_EFFECT table.

ROW_NUM	TRAN_TYPE_ID	ACCT_KEY	EFFECT	JRNL_TYPE	AMOUNT_COLUMN	CF_ID
3	2	23	INCREASE	DEBIT	AMOUNT	
4	2	1	DECREASE	CREDIT	AMOUNT	11

- Long-term business loan

  The long-term business loan increases the Long-term loan (Credit side) and the Checking account (Debit side) by value in the AMOUNT column. The Cash flow classification is 'Add: long-term debt'. The following two rows are added to the TRAN_TYPE_EFFECT table.

ROW_NUM	TRAN_TYPE_ID	ACCT_KEY	EFFECT	JRNL_TYPE	AMOUNT_COLUMN	CF_ID
5	3	11	INCREASE	CREDIT	AMOUNT	
6	3	1	INCREASE	DEBIT	AMOUNT	9

- Long-term loan payment

  The PRINCIPAL column value decreases the Long-term loan account (Credit side). The AMOUNT column value reduces the Checking account (Debit side). The INTEREST column value increases the Loan Interest account (Debit side). Cash movement is classified as 'Less: Repayments of long-term debt'.
  The following three rows are added to the TRAN_TYPE_EFFECT table:

ROW_NUM	TRAN_TYPE_ID	ACCT_KEY	EFFECT	JRNL_TYPE	AMOUNT_COLUMN	CF_ID
7	4	11	DECREASE	DEBIT	CAPITAL	
8	4	21	INCREASE	DEBIT	INTEREST	
9	4	1	DECREASE	CREDIT	AMOUNT	10

- Mortgage loan

  The Mortgage loan increases the accounts, Mortgage loan (Credit side) and Land and property account (Debit side) by the AMOUNT column value.

The following two entries are added to the TRAN_TYPE_EFFECT table:

ROW_NUM	TRAN_TYPE_ID	ACCT_KEY	EFFECT	JRNL_TYPE	AMOUNT_COLUMN	CF_ID
10	5	12	INCREASE	CREDIT	AMOUNT	
11	5	7	INCREASE	DEBIT	AMOUNT	

- Mortgage loan payment

  The Capital column value reduces the Mortgage loan account (Credit side), the INTEREST column value increases the Loan Interest account (Debit side), and the AMOUNT column value reduces the Checking account (Debit side).
  Cash movement is classified as 'Less: Repayments of long-term debt'. The following three entries are added to the TRAN_TYPE_EFFECT table:

ROW_NUM	TRAN_TYPE_ID	ACCT_KEY	EFFECT	JRNL_TYPE	AMOUNT_COLUMN	CF_ID
12	6	12	DECREASE	DEBIT	CAPITAL	
13	6	21	INCREASE	DEBIT	INTEREST	
14	6	1	DECREASE	CREDIT	AMOUNT	10

Asset Management (AM)

The effects of each type of transaction are as follows:

- Computer hardware purchase

  Computer hardware purchase increases the Computer hardware account (Debit side) and reduces the Checking account (Debit side) by the amount specified in the AMOUNT column. The cash movement is classified as 'Purchase of property and equipment'.
  The following rows are added to the TRAN_TYPE_EFFECT table:

ROW_NUM	TRAN_TYPE_ID	ACCT_KEY	EFFECT	JRNL_TYPE	AMOUNT_COLUMN	CF_ID
15	7	5	INCREASE	DEBIT	AMOUNT	
16	7	1	DECREASE	CREDIT	AMOUNT	6

- Office furniture purchase

  Office furniture purchase increases the Office furniture account (Debit side) and reduces the Checking account (Debit side) by the value of the

AMOUNT column. The cash movement is also classified as 'Purchase of property and equipment'.

The following rows are added to the TRAN_TYPE_EFFECT table:

ROW_NUM	TRAN_TYPE_ID	ACCT_KEY	EFFECT	JRNL_TYPE	AMOUNT_COLUMN	CF_ID
17	8	4	INCREASE	DEBIT	AMOUNT	
18	8	1	DECREASE	CREDIT	AMOUNT	6

- Vehicle purchase

  Vehicle purchase increases the Vehicle account (Debit side) and reduces the Checking account (Debit side) by the value of the AMOUNT column. The cash movement is also classified as 'Purchase of property and equipment'.

  The TRAN_TYPE_EFFECT table has the following rows added:

ROW_NUM	TRAN_TYPE_ID	ACCT_KEY	EFFECT	JRNL_TYPE	AMOUNT_COLUMN	CF_ID
19	9	6	INCREASE	DEBIT	AMOUNT	
20	9	1	DECREASE	CREDIT	AMOUNT	6

Accounts payable (AP)

The effects of each type of transaction are as follows:

- Utility bill

  The utility bill transaction type increases the Utilities account (Debit side) and the Accounts Payable account (Credit side).

  The following rows are added to the TRAN_TYPE_EFFECT table:

ROW_NUM	TRAN_TYPE_ID	ACCT_KEY	EFFECT	JRNL_TYPE	AMOUNT_COLUMN	CF_ID
21	10	8	INCREASE	CREDIT	AMOUNT	
22	10	18	INCREASE	DEBIT	AMOUNT	

- Utility bill payment

  The utility bill payment transaction type decreases the Accounts Payable account (Credit side) and the Checking account (Debit side).

  The cash movement is classified as 'Cash paid for other operating expenses'. The following rows are added to the TRAN_TYPE_EFFECT table:

ROW_NUM	TRAN_TYPE_ID	ACCT_KEY	EFFECT	JRNL_TYPE	AMOUNT_COLUMN	CF_ID
23	11	8	DECREASE	DEBIT	AMOUNT	
24	11	1	DECREASE	CREDIT	AMOUNT	5

- Office rent payment

  Office rent payment transaction type increases the Office rent account (Debit side) and decreases the Checking account (Debit side). The cash movement classification is also 'Cash paid for other operating expenses'. The following rows are added to the TRAN_TYPE_EFFECT table:

ROW_NUM	TRAN_TYPE_ID	ACCT_KEY	EFFECT	JRNL_TYPE	AMOUNT_COLUMN	CF_ID
25	12	16	INCREASE	DEBIT	AMOUNT	
26	12	1	DECREASE	CREDIT	AMOUNT	5

- Travel/Fuel expenses payment

  The Travel/Fuel expenses payment transaction increases the Travel account (Debit side) and decreases the Checking account (Debit side). The cash movement classification is also 'Cash paid for other operating expenses'.
  The following rows are added to the TRAN_TYPE_EFFECT table:

ROW_NUM	TRAN_TYPE_ID	ACCT_KEY	EFFECT	JRNL_TYPE	AMOUNT_COLUMN	CF_ID
27	13	19	INCREASE	DEBIT	AMOUNT	
28	13	1	DECREASE	CREDIT	AMOUNT	5

- Office sundries payment

  The office sundries payment transaction increases the Office sundries account (Debit side) and decreases the Checking account (Debit side). The cash movement classification is also 'Cash paid for other operating expenses'.
  The following rows are added to the TRAN_TYPE_EFFECT table:

ROW_NUM	TRAN_TYPE_ID	ACCT_KEY	EFFECT	JRNL_TYPE	AMOUNT_COLUMN	CF_ID
29	14	20	INCREASE	DEBIT	AMOUNT	
30	14	1	DECREASE	CREDIT	AMOUNT	5

Accounts receivable (AR)

The effects of the types of transactions are as follows:

- Customer invoice

  A customer invoice transaction increases the Accounts Receivable account (Debit side) and the Consultancy Revenue account (Credit side). The following rows are added to the TRAN_TYPE_EFFECT table:

ROW_NUM	TRAN_TYPE_ID	ACCT_KEY	EFFECT	JRNL_TYPE	AMOUNT_COLUMN	CF_ID
31	15	3	INCREASE	DEBIT	AMOUNT	
32	15	14	INCREASE	CREDIT	AMOUNT	

- Client cash receipt

  The client cash receipt transaction decreases the Accounts receivable account (Debit side) and the Checking account (Debit side). The flow of cash is classified as 'Cash received from customers'.
  The following rows are added to the TRAN_TYPE_EFFECT table:

ROW_NU	TRAN_TYPE_ID	ACCT_KE	EFFECT	JRNL_TYP	AMOUNT_COLUM	CF_ID
33	16	3	DE-	CREDIT	AMOUNT	
34	16	1	INCREASE	DEBIT	AMOUNT	1

Payroll (PAY)

The effects of each type of transaction are as follows:

- Monthly payroll

  Monthly payroll increases three accounts: Staff salaries (Debit side), Income tax payable (Credit side), and Net Pay (Credit side).
  The following rows are added to the TRAN_TYPE_EFFECT table:

ROW_NUM	TRAN_TYPE_ID	ACCT_KEY	EFFECT	JRNL_TYPE	AMOUNT_COLUMN	CF_ID
35	17	17	INCREASE	DEBIT	AMOUNT	
36	17	9	INCREASE	CREDIT	INCOME_TAX	
37	17	10	INCREASE	CREDIT	NET_PAY	

- Income tax payment

  Income tax payment decreases the Income tax payable account (Credit side) and the Checking account (Debit side). The cash flow is categorised as 'Cash paid for Income Tax'.
  The following rows are added to the TRAN_TYPE_EFFECT table:

ROW_NUM	TRAN_TYPE_ID	ACCT_KEY	EFFECT	JRNL_TYPE	AMOUNT_COLUMN	CF_ID
38	18	9	DECREASE	DEBIT	AMOUNT	
39	18	1	DECREASE	CREDIT	AMOUNT	

- Total net salary payment

  The total net salary payment transaction type decreases the Net Pay account (Credit side) and the Checking account (Debit side). Cash movement is categorised as 'Cash paid to Employees'
  The following rows are added to the TRAN_TYPE_EFFECT table:

ROW_NUM	TRAN_TYPE_ID	ACCT_KEY	EFFECT	JRNL_TYPE	AMOUNT_COLUMN	CF_ID
40	19	10	DECREASE	DEBIT	AMOUNT	
41	19	1	DECREASE	CREDIT	AMOUNT	3

Banking (BNK)

The effects of each type of transaction are as follows:

- Transfer to Savings account

  Transfer to Savings account decreases the Checking account (Debit side) and increases the Savings account (Debit side). The inter-account movement of cash does not affect the overall cash flow.
  The following rows are added to the TRAN_TYPE_EFFECT table:

ROW_NUM	TRAN_TYPE_ID	ACCT_KEY	EFFECT	JRNL_TYPE	AMOUNT_COLUMN	CF_ID
42	20	1	DECREASE	CREDIT	AMOUNT	
43	20	2	INCREASE	DEBIT	AMOUNT	

- Transfer to Checking account

  Transfer to the checking account decreases the Savings account (Debit side) and increases the Checking account (Debit side).

The following rows are added to the TRAN_TYPE_EFFECT table:

ROW_NUM	TRAN_TYPE_ID	ACCT_KEY	EFFECT	JRNL_TYPE	AMOUNT_COLUMN	CF_ID
44	21	2	DECREASE	CREDIT	AMOUNT	
45	21	1	INCREASE	DEBIT	AMOUNT	

- Bank charges payment

  The bank charges payment increases the Bank charges account (Debit side) and decreases the Checking account (Debit side). The cash movement is categorised as 'Cash paid for other operating expenses'.
  The following rows are added to the TRAN_TYPE_EFFECT table:

ROW_NUM	TRAN_TYPE_ID	ACCT_KEY	EFFECT	JRNL_TYPE	AMOUNT_COLUMN	CF_ID
46	22	22	INCREASE	DEBIT	AMOUNT	
47	22	1	DECREASE	CREDIT	AMOUNT	5

- Interest earned

  The Interest earned transaction increases the accounts, Interest earned (Credit side) and Savings account (Debit side). The movement of cash is categorised as 'Interest received'.
  The following rows are added to the TRAN_TYPE_EFFECT table:

ROW_NUM	TRAN_TYPE_ID	ACCT_KEY	EFFECT	JRNL_TYPE	AMOUNT_COLUMN	CF_ID
48	23	15	INCREASE	CREDIT	AMOUNT	
49	23	2	INCREASE	DEBIT	AMOUNT	2

CHAPTER 6

Transaction processing code

The data flow diagram below illustrates the movement of data from the six modules discussed through three processes and its storage in three states: transaction, journal, and ledger.

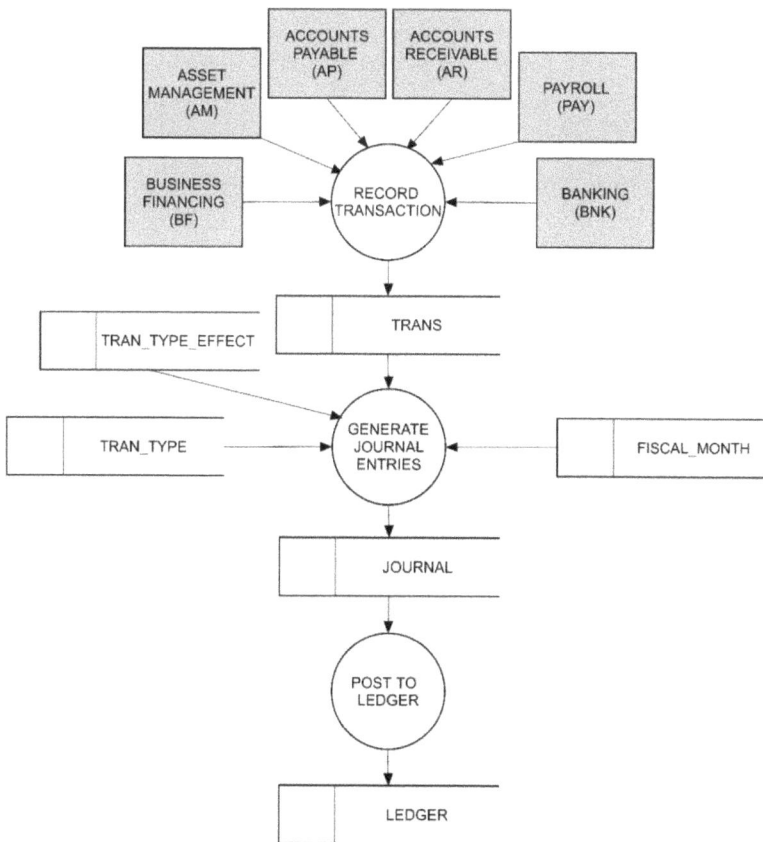

A basic stored procedure, sp_Process_Trans, controls the data flow in the SOKO database. The procedure accepts details of a transaction as parameters from each module and executes three processes one after another, as illustrated in the listing below:

```
CREATE PROCEDURE sp_Process_Trans
        @TRAN_TYPE_ID        INT,
        @TRAN_DATE           DATE,
        @REF_ID              VARCHAR(15),
        @AMOUNT              MONEY,
        @INTEREST            MONEY = NULL,
        @PRINCIPAL           MONEY = NULL,
        @INCOME_TAX          MONEY = NULL,
        @NET_PAY             MONEY = NULL
AS
BEGIN
        DECLARE  @JRNL_NUM    INT

RECORD_TRANS:

        EXEC @JRNL_NUM = sp_Record_Trans
                @TRAN_TYPE_ID,
                @TRAN_DATE,
                @REF_ID,
                @AMOUNT,
                @INTEREST,
                @PRINCIPAL,
                @INCOME_TAX,
                @NET_PAY

GENERATE_JOURNAL_ENTRIES:

        EXEC sp_Generate_Journal_Entries @JRNL_NUM

UPDATE_LEDGER:

        EXEC sp_Post_To_Ledger @JRNL_NUM

END
```

The three processes executed are as follows:

1. Record transaction

   Transaction details are passed as parameters to the stored procedure, sp_Record_Trans. The procedure creates an entry in the table TRANS, and generates and returns a unique journal number for the transaction, as shown in the listing below:

```
CREATE PROCEDURE sp_Record_Trans
    @TRAN_TYPE_ID            INT,
    @TRAN_DATE               DATE,
    @REF_ID                  VARCHAR(15),
    @AMOUNT                  MONEY,
    @INTEREST                MONEY = NULL,
    @PRINCIPAL               MONEY = NULL,
    @INCOME_TAX              MONEY = NULL,
    @NET_PAY                 MONEY = NULL
AS


BEGIN
    DECLARE @JRNL_NUM        BIGINT

    INSERT
    TRANS(TRAN_DATE, TRAN_TYPE_ID, REF_ID, AMOUNT, INTEREST,
          PRINCIPAL, INCOME_TAX, NET_PAY)
    SELECT
          @TRAN_DATE, @TRAN_TYPE_ID, @REF_ID, @AMOUNT,
          @INTEREST, @PRINCIPAL, @INCOME_TAX, @NET_PAY

    SET @JRNL_NUM = @@IDENTITY

    RETURN @JRNL_NUM

END
```

2. Generate journal entries

The unique journal number for each transaction is passed to the procedure, sp_Generate_Journal_Entries, that uses the tables TRANS, TRAN_TYPE, TRAN_TYPE_EFFECT, and FISCAL_MONTH as input to generate journal entries, as shown in the listing below:

```
CREATE PROCEDURE [dbo].[sp_Generate_Journal_Entries]
    @JRNL_NUM          BIGINT
AS
```

```
BEGIN

JOURNAL_ENTRIES:

    INSERT
            JOURNAL
    (
            JRNL_NUM,
            ACCT_KEY,
            TRAN_DATE,
            REF_ID,
            MNTH_ID,
            NARRATIVE,
            DEBIT,
            CREDIT,
            CF_ID
    )
    SELECT
            T.JRNL_NUM,
            TTE.ACCT_KEY,
            T.TRAN_DATE,
            T.REF_ID,
            FM.MNTH_ID,
            TT.TRAN_TYPE AS NARRATIVE,
            CASE WHEN TTE.JRNL_TYPE = 'DEBIT' THEN
                    CASE TTE.AMOUNT_COLUMN
                        WHEN 'AMOUNT' THEN T.AMOUNT
                        WHEN 'INTEREST' THEN T.INTEREST
                        WHEN 'PRINCIPAL' THEN T.PRINCIPAL
                        WHEN 'INCOME_TAX' THEN
T.INCOME_TAX
                        WHEN 'NET_PAY' THEN T.NET_PAY
                    END
                ELSE
                    NULL END AS DEBIT,
            CASE WHEN TTE.JRNL_TYPE = 'CREDIT' THEN
                    CASE TTE.AMOUNT_COLUMN
                        WHEN 'AMOUNT' THEN T.AMOUNT
                        WHEN 'INTEREST' THEN T.INTEREST
                        WHEN 'PRINCIPAL' THEN T.PRINCIPAL
                        WHEN 'INCOME_TAX' THEN
T.INCOME_TAX
                        WHEN 'NET_PAY' THEN T.NET_PAY
                    END
                ELSE
                    NULL END AS CREDIT,
```

```
            TTE.CF_ID
    FROM
            TRANS AS T
    JOIN
            TRAN_TYPE AS TT
            ON    T.TRAN_TYPE_ID = TT.TRAN_TYPE_ID
    JOIN
            TRAN_TYPE_EFFECT AS TTE
            ON    T.TRAN_TYPE_ID = TTE.TRAN_TYPE_ID
    JOIN
            FISCAL_MONTH AS FM
            ON    T.TRAN_DATE BETWEEN FM.START_DATE AND
                  FM.END_DATE
    WHERE
            T.JRNL_NUM = @JRNL_NUM

END
```

3. Post to Ledger

The third stored procedure executed is sp_Post_To_Ledger which up-dates the LEDGER from the journal entries created in the last stage, as il-lustrated in the listing below:

```
CREATE PROCEDURE sp_Post_To_Ledger
    @JRNL_NUM         BIGINT
AS

BEGIN
;
    WITH JRNL AS
        (SELECT
                ACCT_KEY, MNTH_ID, DEBIT, CREDIT
         FROM
                JOURNAL
         WHERE
                JRNL_NUM = @JRNL_NUM
        )
    MERGE LEDGER AS L
    USING JRNL AS J
    ON    (L.ACCT_KEY = J.ACCT_KEY AND
           L.MNTH_ID = J.MNTH_ID)
    WHEN MATCHED
      THEN
          UPDATE
```

```
                    SET DEBIT = CASE WHEN ISNULL(L.DEBIT, 0) +
ISNULL(J.DEBIT, 0)
> ISNULL(L.CREDIT, 0) + ISNULL(J.CREDIT, 0) THEN
                                    (ISNULL(L.DEBIT, 0) +
ISNULL(J.DEBIT, 0)) - (ISNULL(L.CREDIT, 0) + ISNULL(J.CREDIT, 0))
ELSE NULL END,
                    CREDIT = CASE WHEN ISNULL(L.CREDIT, 0)
+ ISNULL(J.CREDIT, 0) > ISNULL(L.DEBIT, 0) + ISNULL(J.DEBIT, 0)
THEN
                                    (ISNULL(L.CREDIT, 0) +
ISNULL(J.CREDIT, 0)) - (ISNULL(L.DEBIT, 0) + ISNULL(J.DEBIT, 0))
ELSE NULL END

    WHEN NOT MATCHED BY TARGET
        THEN
                INSERT(ACCT_KEY, MNTH_ID, DEBIT, CREDIT)
                VALUES(J.ACCT_KEY, J.MNTH_ID, ISNULL(J.DEBIT,
0), ISNULL(J.CREDIT, 0))
    ;
END
```

CHAPTER 7

Processing transactions

This chapter takes accounting concepts on a test drive. T-SQL code is executed to demonstrate the application of stored rules in transaction processing and to populate output tables.

The main stored procedure, sp_Process_Trans, which was introduced in the last chapter, is executed for each of the following transactions that occurred in the business's first month of trading.

1. Owner cash contribution

    On April 2, 2023, C. Murewa started a business with £15,000 of his savings, which he deposited into the business checking account with reference OC-1.

    The Business Financing module passes the following parameters to the transaction processing procedure:

    ```
    exec sp_Process_Trans
        @TRAN_TYPE_ID      = 1,
        @TRAN_DATE         = '2 Apr 2023',
        @REF_ID            = 'OC-1',
        @AMOUNT            = 15000.00
    ```

    The following three output tables are populated. A subset of the columns is listed below:

- TRANS

TRAN_DATE	TRAN_TYPE_ID	REF_ID	AMOUNT	JRNL_NUM
2023-04-02	1	OC-1	15000.00	101

- JOURNAL

JRNL_NUM	ACCT_KEY	REF_ID	MNTH_ID	NARRATIVE	DEBIT	CREDIT	CF_ID
101	13	OC-1	202401	Owner cash contribution		15000.00	
101	1	OC-1	202401	Owner cash contribution	15000.00		8

- LEDGER

ROW_NUM	ACCT_KEY	MNTH_ID	DEBIT	CREDIT
1	13	202401		15000.00
2	1	202401	15000.00	

2. Long-term business loan

On April 3, 2023, the bank granted a five-year loan of £30,000, which was paid into the business checking account, reference LTL-1.

The Business Financing module passes the following parameters to the transaction processing procedure:

```
exec sp_Process_Trans
    @TRAN_TYPE_ID    = 3,
    @TRAN_DATE       = '3 Apr 2023',
    @REF_ID          = 'LTL-1',
    @AMOUNT          = 30000.00
```

The three output tables are populated and updated as follows:

- TRANS

TRAN_DATE	TRAN_TYPE_ID	REF_ID	AMOUNT	JRNL_NUM
2023-04-03	3	LTL-1	30000.00	102

- JOURNAL

JRNL_NUM	ACCT_KEY	REF_ID	MNTH_ID	NARRATIVE	DEBIT	CREDIT	CF_ID
102	11	LTL-1	202401	Long-term business loan		30000.00	
102	1	LTL-1	202401	Long-term business loan	30000.00		9

- LEDGER

ROW_NUM	ACCT_KEY	MNTH_ID	DEBIT	CREDIT
2	1	202401	45000.00	
3	11	202401		30000.00

3. Office rent

The premises are rented on April 4, 2023, for £1,600 per month. The first month's rent is paid by bank card, referenced as OR-1, and a direct debit is set up to collect the rent on the 4th of each month thereafter.

The Accounts Payable and Expenses module passes the following parameters to the transaction processing procedure:

```
exec sp_Process_Trans
    @TRAN_TYPE_ID      = 12,
    @TRAN_DATE         = '4 Apr 2023',
    @REF_ID            = 'OR-1',
    @AMOUNT            = 1600.00
```

The three output tables are populated and updated as follows:

- TRANS

TRAN_DATE	TRAN_TYPE_ID	REF_ID	AMOUNT	JRNL_NUM
2023-04-04	12	OR-1	1600.00	103

- JOURNAL

JRNL_NUM	ACCT_KEY	REF_ID	MNTH_ID	NARRATIVE	DEBIT	CREDIT	CF_ID
103	16	OR-1	202401	Office rent payment	1600.00		
103	1	OR-1	202401	Office rent payment		1600.00	5

- LEDGER

ROW_NUM	ACCT_KEY	MNTH_ID	DEBIT	CREDIT
2	1	202401	43400.00	
4	16	202401	1600.00	

4. Office furniture purchase

    Pelhams Office Furniture Limited delivers desks and chairs worth £4,560.00, paid for by bank card on April 4, 2023, reference 231.

    The Asset Management module passes the following parameters to the transaction processing procedure:

    ```
    exec sp_Process_Trans
        @TRAN_TYPE_ID      = 8,
        @TRAN_DATE         = '4 Apr 2023',
        @REF_ID            = '231',
        @AMOUNT            = 4560.00
    ```

    The output tables are populated and updated as follows:

    *   TRANS

TRAN_DATE	TRAN_TYPE_ID	REF_ID	AMOUNT	JRNL_NUM
2023-04-04	8	231	4560.00	104

    *   JOURNAL

JRNL_NUM	ACCT_KEY	REF_ID	MNTH_ID	NARRATIVE	DEBIT	CREDIT	CF_ID
104	4	231	202401	Office furniture purchase	4560.00		
104	1	231	202401	Office furniture purchase		4560.00	6

    *   LEDGER

ROW_NUM	ACCT_KEY	MNTH_ID	DEBIT	CREDIT
2	1	202401	38840.00	
5	4	202401	4560.00	

5. Computer hardware purchase

    Computer hardware equipment worth £11,400 was purchased from MemSys Computer Systems and paid for by bank card on April 5, 2023, reference 232.

    The Asset Management module passes the following parameters to the transaction processing procedure:

```
exec sp_Process_Trans
    @TRAN_TYPE_ID        = 7,
    @TRAN_DATE           = '5 Apr 2023',
    @REF_ID              = '232',
    @AMOUNT              = 11400.00
```

The output tables are populated and updated as follows:

- TRANS

TRAN_DATE	TRAN_TYPE_ID	REF_ID	AMOUNT	JRNL_NUM
2023-04-05	7	232	11400.00	105

- JOURNAL

JRNL_NUM	ACCT_KEY	REF_ID	MNTH_ID	NARRATIVE	DEBIT	CREDIT	CF_ID
105	5	232	202401	Computer hardware purchase	11400.00		
105	1	232	202401	Computer hardware purchase		11400.00	6

- LEDGER

ROW_NUM	ACCT_KEY	MNTH_ID	DEBIT	CREDIT
2	1	202401	27440.00	
6	5	202401	11400.00	

6. Transfer to Savings account

A savings account was opened on April 6, 2023, and £ 5,000 was transferred from the checking account, reference 24451.

The Banking module passes the following parameters to the transaction processing procedure:

```
exec sp_Process_Trans
    @TRAN_TYPE_ID        = 20,
    @TRAN_DATE           = '6 Apr 2023',
    @REF_ID              = '24451',
    @AMOUNT              = 5000.00
```

The output tables are populated and updated as follows:

- TRANS

TRAN_DATE	TRAN_TYPE_ID	REF_ID	AMOUNT	JRNL_NUM
2023-04-06	20	24451	5000.00	106

- JOURNAL

JRNL_NUM	ACCT_KEY	REF_ID	MNTH_ID	NARRATIVE	DEBIT	CREDIT	CF_ID
106	1	24451	202401	Transfer to Savings account		5000.00	
106	2	24451	202401	Transfer to Savings account	5000.00		

- LEDGER

ROW_NUM	ACCT_KEY	MNTH_ID	DEBIT	CREDIT
2	1	202401	22440.00	
7	2	202401	5000.00	

7. Customer invoice

On April 11, 2023, an invoice of £14,600 was generated for consultancy work and emailed to M&M, reference 1001.

The Accounts Receivable module passes the details to the transaction processing procedure as follows:

```
exec sp_Process_Trans
    @TRAN_TYPE_ID   = 15,
    @TRAN_DATE      = '11 Apr 2023',
    @REF_ID         = '1001',
    @AMOUNT         = 14600.00
```

The output tables are populated and updated as follows:

- TRANS

TRAN_DATE	TRAN_TYPE_ID	REF_ID	AMOUNT	JRNL_NUM
2023-04-11	15	1001	14600.00	107

- JOURNAL

JRNL_NUM	ACCT_KEY	REF_ID	MNTH_ID	NARRATIVE	DEBIT	CREDIT	CF_ID
107	3	101	202401	Customer invoice	14600.00		
107	14	101	202401	Customer invoice		14600.00	

- LEDGER

ROW_NUM	ACCT_KEY	MNTH_ID	DEBIT	CREDIT
8	3	202401	14600.00	
9	14	202401		14600.00

8. Client cash receipt

On April 13, 2023, M&M transferred £4,750.00 into the checking account as part of the payment for the amount they owed, reference 501.

The Accounts Receivable module passes the details to the transaction processing procedure as follows:

```
exec sp_Process_Trans
    @TRAN_TYPE_ID   = 16,
    @TRAN_DATE      = '13 Apr 2023',
    @REF_ID         = '501',
    @AMOUNT         = 4750.00
```

The output tables are populated and updated as follows:

- TRANS

TRAN_DATE	TRAN_TYPE_ID	REF_ID	AMOUNT	JRNL_NUM
2023-04-11	16	501	4750.00	108

- JOURNAL

JRNL_NUM	ACCT_KEY	REF_ID	MNTH_ID	NARRATIVE	DEBIT	CREDIT	CF_ID
108	3	501	202401	Client cash receipt		4750.00	
108	1	501	202401	Client cash receipt	4750.00		1

- LEDGER

ROW_NUM	ACCT_KEY	MNTH_ID	DEBIT	CREDIT
2	1	202401	27190.00	
8	3	202401	9850.00	

9. Utility bill

A Utility bill (Electricity and Gas) for £101 was received on April 24, 2023, reference UB-4.

The Accounts Payable and Expenses module passes the details to the transaction processing procedure as follows:

```
exec sp_Process_Trans
    @TRAN_TYPE_ID   = 10,
    @TRAN_DATE      = '24 Apr 2023',
    @REF_ID         = 'UB-4',
    @AMOUNT         = 101.00
```

The output tables are populated and updated as follows:
- TRANS

TRAN_DATE	TRAN_TYPE_ID	REF_ID	AMOUNT	JRNL_NUM
2023-04-24	10	UB-4	101.00	109

- JOURNAL

JRNL_NUM	ACCT_KEY	REF_ID	MNTH_ID	NARRATIVE	DEBIT	CREDIT	CF_ID
109	8	UB-4	202401	Utility bill		101.00	
109	18	UB-4	202401	Utility bill	101.00		

- LEDGER

ROW_NUM	ACCT_KEY	MNTH_ID	DEBIT	CREDIT
10	8	202401		101.00
11	18	202401	101.00	

10. Monthly Payroll

The current month's payroll is run on April 25, 2023. The gross pay is £12,500.00; the calculated income tax is £4,500.00, and the net pay is £8,000.00 (reference 04/24).

The Payroll Module passes payroll totals to the transaction processing procedure as follows:

```
exec sp_Process_Trans
    @TRAN_TYPE_ID   = 17,
    @TRAN_DATE      = '25 Apr 2023',
    @REF_ID         = '04/24',
    @AMOUNT         = 12500.00,
    @INCOME_TAX     = 4500.00,
    @NET_PAY        = 8000.00
```

The output tables are populated and updated as follows:

- TRANS

TRAN_DATE	TRAN_TYPE_ID	REF_ID	AMOUNT	INCOME_TAX	NET_PAY	JRNL_NUM
2023-04-25	17	04/24	12500.00	4500.00	8000.00	110

- JOURNAL

JRNL_NUM	ACCT_KEY	REF_ID	MNTH_ID	NARRATIVE	DEBIT	CREDIT	CF_ID
110	17	04/24	202401	Monthly payroll	12500.00		
110	9	04/24	202401	Monthly payroll		4500.00	
110	10	04/24	202401	Monthly payroll		8000.00	

- LEDGER

ROW_NUM	ACCT_KEY	MNTH_ID	DEBIT	CREDIT
12	17	202401	12500.00	
13	9	202401		4500.00
14	10	202401		8000.00

11. Net salary payment

The April 2023 total net pay of £ 8,000 is transferred to employees' bank accounts on April 26, 2023, reference 0424.

The Payroll module passes the details to the transaction processing procedure as follows:

```
exec sp_Process_Trans
    @TRAN_TYPE_ID    = 19,
    @TRAN_DATE       = '26 Apr 2023',
    @REF_ID          = '0424',
    @AMOUNT          = 8000.00
```

The output tables are populated and updated as follows:

- TRANS

TRAN_DATE	TRAN_TYPE_ID	REF_ID	AMOUNT	JRNL_NUM
2023-04-26	19	0424	8000.00	111

- JOURNAL

JRNL_NUM	ACCT_KEY	REF_ID	MNTH_ID	NARRATIVE	DEBIT	CREDIT	CF_ID
111	10	0424	202401	Net salary payment	8000.00		
111	1	0424	202401	Net salary payment		8000.00	3

- LEDGER

ROW_NUM	ACCT_KEY	MNTH_ID	DEBIT	CREDIT
2	1	202401	19190.00	
14	10	202401		

12. Income tax payment

On April 26, 2023, the income tax payable of £4,500 was paid, reference 0424.

The Payroll module passes the details to the transaction processing procedure as follows:

```
exec sp_Process_Trans
    @TRAN_TYPE_ID    = 18,
    @TRAN_DATE       = '26 Apr 2023',
    @REF_ID          = '0424',
    @AMOUNT          = 4500.00
```

The output tables are populated and updated as follows:

- TRANS

TRAN_DATE	TRAN_TYPE_ID	REF_ID	AMOUNT	JRNL_NUM
2023-04-26	18	0424	4500.00	112

- JOURNAL

JRNL_NUM	ACCT_KEY	REF_ID	MNTH_ID	NARRATIVE	DEBIT	CREDIT	CF_ID
112	9	0424	202401	Income tax payment	4500.00		
112	1	0424	202401	Income tax payment		4500.00	4

- LEDGER

ROW_NUM	ACCT_KEY	MNTH_ID	DEBIT	CREDIT
2	1	202401	14690.00	
13	9	202401		

13. Long-term loan payment

On April 30, 2023, a long-term loan payment of £577.77 is made by direct bank debit, representing £500.00 principal and £77.77 loan interest, reference LP-1.

The Business Financing module passes the details to the transaction processing procedure as follows:

```
exec sp_Process_Trans
     @TRAN_TYPE_ID   = 4,
     @TRAN_DATE      = '30 Apr 2023',
     @REF_ID         = 'LP-1',
     @AMOUNT         = 577.77,
     @INTEREST       = 77.77,
     @PRINCIPAL      = 500.00
```

The output tables are populated and updated as follows:

- TRANS

TRAN_DATE	TRAN_TYPE_ID	REF_ID	AMOUNT	INTEREST	PRINCIPAL	JRNL_NUM
2023-04-30	4	LP-1	577.77	77.77	500.00	113

- JOURNAL

JRNL_NUM	ACCT_KEY	REF_ID	MNTH_ID	NARRATIVE	DEBIT	CREDIT	CF_ID
113	11	LP-1	202401	Long-term loan payment	500.00		
113	21	LP-1	202401	Long-term loan payment	77.77		
113	1	LP-1	202401	Long-term loan payment		577.77	10

- LEDGER

ROW_NUM	ACCT_KEY	MNTH_ID	DEBIT	CREDIT
2	1	202401	14112.23	
3	11	202401		29500.00
15	21	202401	77.77	

CHAPTER 8

Data Verification

The listing below shows the month's effective changes to the balances of each account after the 13 transactions processed in April 2023.

ROW_NUM	ACCT_KEY	MNTH_ID	DEBIT	CREDIT
1	13	202401		15000.00
2	1	202401	14112.23	
3	11	202401		29500.00
4	16	202401	1600.00	
5	4	202401	4560.00	
6	5	202401	11400.00	
7	2	202401	5000.00	
8	3	202401	9850.00	
9	14	202401		14600.00
10	8	202401		101.00
11	18	202401	101.00	
12	17	202401	12500.00	
13	9	202401		
14	10	202401		
15	21	202401	77.77	

Is this a correct representation of the transactions that have been processed?

Data Quality

The adage "garbage in, garbage out" underscores the importance of data quality. The consequences of incorrect or incomplete data are, at best, an inconvenience that hinders informed decision-making. In some instances, inaccurate financial reporting can damage the credibility of a business.

The quality of accounting data held must be verified before it is used. At the very minimum, the data must pass the following quality tests:

- The journal and the ledger must accurately reflect all transactions. The data must be traceable from summary records in the ledger to the source transactions.
- Validation starts at transaction data entry by ensuring sufficient information is collected to create journal entries or to rebuild the journal table in case of data corruption or loss.
- Every journal entry must reference the source transaction, and the amount debited for each transaction must correspond to the amount credited.
- The journal's monthly aggregates of each account must be in sync with the monthly movements in the ledger.

Trial balance

The Trial balance is a report that helps verify accounting data. It lists the ending balance of each account at a specific date, usually at the end of the month.

As shown below, an account's side of the equation determines how the balance is calculated.

Side of the equation	Balance calculation
Left (Debit)	Debit – Credit
Right (Credit)	Credit – Debit

The following resultset, retrieved from the LEDGER table, shows the balances of the accounts after the transactions processed to date:

ACCT_ID	ACCT_NAME	DEBIT	CREDIT
1000	Checking account	14112.23	
1010	Savings account	5000.00	
1020	Accounts receivable	9850.00	
1500	Office furniture	4560.00	
1510	Computer hardware	11400.00	
2000	Accounts payable		101.00
2500	Long-term loan		29500.00
3000	Capital		15000.00
4000	Consultancy Revenue		14600.00
5000	Office rent	1600.00	
5010	Staff salaries	12500.00	
5020	Utilities	101.00	
5040	Loan Interest	77.77	

The resultset is used to prepare the following Trial balance report:

	Murewa Consultancy		
	Trial Balance		
	April 30, 2023		
Number	Account	Debit	Credit
1000	Checking account	£14,112.23	
1010	Savings account	5,000.00	
1020	Accounts receivable	9,850.00	
1500	Office furniture	4,560.00	
1510	Computer hardware	11,400.00	
2000	Accounts payable		£101.00
2500	Long-term loan		29,500.00
3000	Capital		15,000.00
4000	Consultancy Revenue		14,600.00
5000	Office rent	1,600.00	
5010	Staff salaries	12,500.00	
5020	Utilities	101.00	
5040	Loan Interest	77.77	
Totals		£59,201.00	£59,201.00

An example of T-SQL data retrieval code for the Trial balance is listed below:

```
DECLARE    @MNTH_ID   INT = 202401

SELECT
     A.ACCT_ID,
     A.ACCT_NAME,
     SUM(CASE WHEN AE.SIDE = 'DEBIT'  THEN
        ISNULL(L.DEBIT, 0) - ISNULL(L.CREDIT, 0) END) AS DEBIT,
     SUM(CASE WHEN AE.SIDE = 'CREDIT'  THEN
        ISNULL(L.CREDIT, 0) - ISNULL(L.DEBIT, 0) END) AS CREDIT
FROM
     LEDGER AS L
```

```
JOIN
      ACCOUNT AS A
      ON     L.ACCT_KEY = A.ACCT_KEY
JOIN
      ACCOUNTING_EQUATION AS AE
      ON     A.ELEMENT_ID = AE.ELEMENT_ID
WHERE
      L.MNTH_ID BETWEEN ROUND(@MNTH_ID, -2) AND
@MNTH_ID
GROUP BY
      A.ACCT_ID,
      A.ACCT_NAME
HAVING
      SUM(CASE WHEN AE.SIDE = 'DEBIT' THEN
       ISNULL(L.DEBIT, 0) - ISNULL(L.CREDIT, 0) END) <> 0
      OR
      SUM(CASE WHEN AE.SIDE = 'CREDIT' THEN
       ISNULL(L.CREDIT, 0) - ISNULL(L.DEBIT, 0) END) <> 0
ORDER BY
      A.ACCT_ID
```

The above Trial balance communicates the following:

- Every debit entry has a corresponding credit entry
- Total balances of accounts on the debit (left) side are equal to the total balances of accounts on the credit side of the accounting equation.

Limitations of the trial balance

A trial balance cannot guarantee the accuracy of the data held. It confirms that double-entry rules were correctly applied to process transactions in a specific period. The report cannot detect the following errors:
- Compensation errors
- Transposition
- Wrong values

The quality of accounting data is largely dependent on the accuracy of data entry.

CHAPTER 9

Financial Statements Preparation

This chapter tests the SOKO data model for completeness, accuracy, consistency, and timeliness. The higher the quality of the data model, the easier and faster it should be to retrieve information to prepare financial statements.

Income Statement

Below is an income statement example based on transactions processed in April 2023 and through the current year-to-date.

Murewa Consultancy Income Statement for month ending April 30, 2023	
Revenues	
Consultancy Revenue	14,600.00
Total Revenues	14,600.00
Expenses	
Office rent	1,600.00
Gross Pay	12,500.00
Utilities	101.00
Loan Interest	77.77
Total Expenses	14,278.77
Net Income (Loss)	321.23

The report shows the difference between revenue and expenses. So, only revenue and expenses accounts are retrieved using the following T-SQL code:

```
DECLARE      @MNTH_ID  INT = 202401

SELECT
      AE.ELEMENT, A.ACCT_ID, A.ACCT_NAME,
      SUM(CASE WHEN L.MNTH_ID = @MNTH_ID THEN
            CASE WHEN AE.SIDE = 'Debit' THEN
                  ISNULL(L.DEBIT, 0) - ISNULL(L.CREDIT, 0) ELSE
                  ISNULL(L.CREDIT, 0) - ISNULL(L.DEBIT, 0) END
END) AS AMOUNT,
      SUM(CASE WHEN AE.SIDE = 'Debit' THEN
                  ISNULL(L.DEBIT, 0) - ISNULL(L.CREDIT, 0) ELSE
                  ISNULL(L.CREDIT, 0) - ISNULL(L.DEBIT, 0) END) AS
AMOUNT_YTD
FROM
      ACCOUNTING_EQUATION AS AE
JOIN
      ACCOUNT AS A
      ON    AE.ELEMENT_ID = A.ELEMENT_ID
JOIN
      LEDGER AS L
      ON    A.ACCT_KEY = L.ACCT_KEY AND
            L.MNTH_ID BETWEEN ROUND(@MNTH_ID, -2) AND
@MNTH_ID
WHERE
      AE.ELEMENT IN ('Revenue', 'Expenses') AND
      L.MNTH_ID BETWEEN ROUND(@MNTH_ID, -2) AND
@MNTH_ID

GROUP BY
      AE.ELEMENT, A.ACCT_ID, A.ACCT_NAME
ORDER BY
      A.ACCT_ID
```

The code retrieves the following resultset:

ELEMENT	ACCT_ID	ACCT_NAME	AMOUNT	AMOUNT_YTD
Revenue	4000	Consultancy Revenue	14600.00	14600.00
Expenses	5000	Office rent	1600.00	1600.00
Expenses	5010	Staff salaries	12500.00	12500.00
Expenses	5020	Utilities	101.00	101.00
Expenses	5040	Loan interest	77.77	77.77

Balance Sheet Statement

The balance sheet statement sample below provides a snapshot of Murewa Consultancy's financial position as of April 30, 2023:

Murewa Consultancy Balance Sheet for the period ending April 30, 2023	
Assets	
Current Assets	
Checking account	14,112.23
Savings account	5,000.00
Accounts receivable	9,850.00
Total Current Assets	**28,962.23**
Long-term Assets	
Office furniture	4,560.00
Computer hardware	11,400.00
Total Long-term Assets	**15,960.00**
Total Assets	**44,922.23**
Liabilities	
Current Liabilities	
Accounts payable	101.00
Total Current Liabilities	**101.00**
Long-term Liabilities	
Long-term Liabilities	29,500.00
Long-term Liabilities	**29,500.00**
Owner's Equity	
Capital	15,000.00
Profit/Loss	321.23
	15,321.23
Total Liabilities and Owner's Equity	**44,922.23**

The following T-SQL code retrieves a snapshot of balance sheet data:

```
DECLARE @MNTH_ID            INT = 202401

SELECT
      AE.ELEMENT,
      CASE WHEN AE.ELEMENT = 'Owner''s Equity' THEN AE.ELEMENT
ELSE BS.CATEGORY END AS CATEGORY,
      CASE WHEN BS.CATEGORY = 'Net Income (Profit/Loss)' THEN
4000 ELSE A.ACCT_ID END AS ACCT_ID,
```

```
        CASE WHEN BS.CATEGORY = 'Net Income (Profit/Loss)' THEN
BS.CATEGORY ELSE A.ACCT_NAME END AS ACCT_NAME,
        SUM(
        CASE WHEN AE.SIDE = 'Debit' THEN
                ISNULL(L.DEBIT, 0) - ISNULL(L.CREDIT, 0) ELSE
                ISNULL(L.CREDIT, 0) - ISNULL(L.DEBIT, 0) END
        ) AS AMOUNT
FROM
        ACCOUNTING_EQUATION AS AE
JOIN
        BS_CATEGORY AS BS
        ON      AE.ELEMENT_ID = BS.ELEMENT_ID
JOIN
        ACCOUNT AS A
        ON      A.CATEGORY_ID = BS.CATEGORY_ID
JOIN
        LEDGER AS L
        ON      A.ACCT_KEY = L.ACCT_KEY
WHERE
        L.MNTH_ID BETWEEN  ROUND(@MNTH_ID, -2) AND
@MNTH_ID
GROUP BY
        AE.ELEMENT,
        CASE WHEN AE.ELEMENT = 'Owner''s Equity' THEN AE.ELEMENT
ELSE BS.CATEGORY END,
        CASE WHEN BS.CATEGORY = 'Net Income (Profit/Loss)' THEN
4000 ELSE A.ACCT_ID END,
        CASE WHEN BS.CATEGORY = 'Net Income (Profit/Loss)' THEN
BS.CATEGORY ELSE A.ACCT_NAME END
HAVING
        SUM(
        CASE WHEN AE.SIDE = 'Debit' THEN
                ISNULL(L.DEBIT, 0) - ISNULL(L.CREDIT, 0) ELSE
                ISNULL(L.CREDIT, 0) - ISNULL(L.DEBIT, 0) END
        ) <> 0.00
```

The following listing is the query's resultset:

ELEMENT	BS_HEADING	ACCT_ID	ACCT_NAME	AMOUNT
Assets	Current Assets	1000	Checking account	14112.23
Assets	Current Assets	1010	Savings account	5000.00
Assets	Current Assets	1020	Accounts receivable	9850.00
Assets	Long-term Assets	1500	Office furniture	4560.00
Assets	Long-term Assets	1510	Computer hardware	11400.00
Liabilities	Current Liabilities	2000	Accounts payable	101.00
Liabilities	Long-term Liabilities	2510	Bank Loan	29500.00
Owner's Equity	Owner's Equity	3000	Capital	15000.00
Owner's Equity	Owner's Equity	4000	Net Income (Profit/Loss)	321.23

Cash Flow Statement

The cash flow statement sample below summarises cash inflows and outflows at the end of April 2023.

Murewa Consultancy Statement of Cash Flows for month ending April 30, 2023	
Opening Balance	0.00
Operating Activities	
Cash received from customers	4,750.00
Cash paid to Employees	-8,000.00
Cash paid for Income Tax	-4,500.00
Cash paid for other operating expenses	-1,600.00
Net cash from Operating Activities (A)	-9,350.00
Investing Activities	
Purchase of property and equipment	-15,960.00
Net cash from Investing Activities (B)	-15,960.00
Financing Activities	
Add: Investment by the owner	15,000.00
Add: long-term debt	30,000.00
Less: Repayments of long-term debt	-577.77
Net cash from Financing Activities ©	44,422.23
Increase / Decrease in cash and cash equivalents (A+B+C)	19,112.23
Ending Cash Balance	19,112.23

The Cash Flow statement retrieves the opening balance from the LEDGER, and obtains cash inflow and outflow details from the JOURNAL, as illustrated in the following T-SQL code:

```
DECLARE      @MNTH_ID          INT = 202401
;
WITH OB AS
(
SELECT
      4 AS ACTIVITY_ID, 'Opening Cash Balance' AS ACTIVITY,
      99 AS CF_ID,
      '' AS CATEGORY, ISNULL(SUM(ISNULL(S.DEBIT, 0) -
ISNULL(S.CREDIT, 0)), 0) AS AMOUNT
FROM
      LEDGER AS S
JOIN
      ACCOUNT AS A
      ON    S.ACCT_KEY = A.ACCT_KEY
WHERE
      A.CCE_IND = 1 AND
      S.MNTH_ID BETWEEN ROUND(@MNTH_ID, -2) AND @MNTH_ID
- 1
)
SELECT
      A.ACTIVITY_ID, A.ACTIVITY + ' Activities' AS ACTIVITY,
      H.CF_ID,
      H.CATEGORY, SUM(ISNULL(S.DEBIT, 0) - ISNULL(S.CREDIT, 0))
AS AMOUNT
FROM
      ACTIVITY AS A
JOIN
      CF_CATEGORY AS H
      ON    A.ACTIVITY_ID = H.ACTIVITY_ID
LEFT JOIN
      JOURNAL AS S
      ON    H.CF_ID = S.CF_ID AND
            S.MNTH_ID = @MNTH_ID
GROUP BY
      A.ACTIVITY_ID, A.ACTIVITY + ' Activities',
      H.CF_ID,
      H.CATEGORY
UNION ALL
SELECT
      ACTIVITY_ID, ACTIVITY, CF_ID, CATEGORY, AMOUNT
FROM
      OB AS A
ORDER BY
      ACTIVITY_ID, CF_ID
```

The SOKO database simplifies what could be a complex query to produce the following resultset:

ACTIVITY_ID	ACTIVITY	CF_ID	CF_HEADING	AMOUNT
1	Operating Activities	1	Cash received from customers	4750.00
1	Operating Activities	2	Interest received	0.00
1	Operating Activities	3	Cash paid to Employees	-8000.00
1	Operating Activities	4	Cash paid for Income Tax	-4500.00
1	Operating Activities	5	Cash paid for other operating expenses	-1600.00
2	Investing Activities	6	Purchase of property and Equipment	-15960.00
2	Investing Activities	7	Sale of property and equipment	0.00
3	Financing Activities	8	Add: Investment by the owner	15000.00
3	Financing Activities	9	Add: long-term debt	30000.00
3	Financing Activities	10	Less: Repayments of long-term debt	-577.77
3	Financing Activities	11	Less: Withdrawals by the owner	0.00
4	Opening Cash Balance	99		0.00

Tracking a transaction to financial statements

Tracking how every transaction transforms each financial statement can be enlightening. How about truncating the tables LEDGER, JOURNAL, and TRANS to start afresh?

Task: Process each transaction in the first month of trading, one at a time, and run the data retrieval code for each financial statement. What do you understand about the data movement from each transaction to the financial statements?

CHAPTER 10

Month-end Process

The month-end process, also known as the month-end close, preserves the month-end-state of each account, enabling retrospective and comparative reporting. Monthly movements of each account are frozen and kept static for each closed month.

The basic month-end process involves the following steps:
- Verifying the validity of the data processed in the month
- Closing the current month
- Preparing interim financial statements
- Opening the following month for processing

Monthly verification of data

Monthly verification of data enables the early identification of data inconsistencies, facilitates the resolution of underlying causes, and ensures that business decisions are based on information prepared from valid data.

Data correction

Finance (or Accounts) teams responsible for the correction of data errors, may use one of the following two methods:

- Reverse each incorrect journal entry, followed by the entry of a second journal that correctly records each transaction.
- Record a journal entry that corrects an erroneous original entry.

The full data set is once again verified before proceeding to the next stage.

Closing a month

To close a month, the MONTH_STATUS column in the FISCAL_MONTH table is set to 'CLOSED', as shown in the listing below:

MNTH_ID	YEAR_ID	START_DATE	END_DATE	COMMENTS	MONTH_STATUS
202401	2024	01/04/2023	30/04/2023		CLOSED
202402	2024	01/05/2023	31/05/2023		
202403	2024	01/06/2023	30/05/2023		

This suspends updates to the JOURNAL and LEDGER tables until the following month is set to OPEN.

Interim financial statements can be generated to provide owners, potential investors, and lenders with up-to-date financial information.

Opening a month

Setting the MONTH_STATUS column in the FISCAL_MONTH table to 'OPEN', as shown below, enables transaction processing of business activities of the period:

MNTH_ID	YEAR_ID	START_DATE	END_DATE	COMMENTS	MONTH_STATUS
202401	2024	01/04/2023	30/04/2023		CLOSED
202402	2024	01/05/2023	31/05/2023		OPEN
202403	2024	01/06/2023	30/05/2023		

CHAPTER 11

Monthly cycles

The monthly accounting cycle encompasses the following:

- Opening the month for processing
- Recording business transactions and application of their effects to accounting
- Data verification and adjustments
- Preparation of interim financial statements
- Closure of the month

So, there will be 12 months of verified data at the end of each fiscal year.

Now that you have gone through the first month's cycle, how about putting your understanding to the test by processing transactions for each of the following 11 months? Repetition accelerates your learning speed and deepens your knowledge.

Task: Assess every business transaction conducted in the remaining months of each year and answer three questions. What type of transaction is it, which module does it originate from, and what details are passed to the transaction processing procedure?

Task: Process each transaction in your database and ensure the three output tables (TRANS, JOURNAL, and LEDGER) are correctly populated. Conduct a month-end process once all transactions for the month are complete. Then, open the following month for processing and repeat the process.

Answers to the questions are in the Appendix.

May 2023

1. The premises rent of £1,600.00 is paid by bank card on May 3, reference PR-2.

2. The Savings account earns interest of £51.23 on May 6, reference 1023.
3. On May 9, a consultancy invoice of £14,600.00 is generated and sent to M&M, reference 772.
4. A payment of £9,850.00 is received from M&M on May 10, reference 512.
5. On May 11, another consultancy invoice of £ 11,200.00 is raised and emailed to Witty Computer Systems, reference 773.
6. An annual sewage and water service bill of £101.00 is received on May 13, reference 254.
7. Payment of £4,500 is received from Witty Computer Systems on May 19, reference 881.
8. The month's payroll is run on May 24. The gross pay is £12,500.00; the calculated income tax is £4,500, and the net pay is £8,000. Reference: 05/24.
9. On May 25, the Income tax of £ 4,500 is paid out, reference 05/24.
10. On the same day, May 25, the total net pay of £ 8,000 is paid out, reference 05/24.
11. On May 29, a water bill of £93.50 is received, reference 1090.
12. An Electricity and Gas Bill for £123.45 is received on May 30, reference 611.
13. On May 31, a long-term loan payment of £577.77 is made by direct bank debit, representing £500.00 principal and £77.77 loan interest, reference LTP-2.
14. Bank charges of £12.50 were collected from the checking account on May 31, reference BC1.

Changes to the balances (increases and decreases) of the accounts affected are recorded in the LEDGER table as follows:

ROW_NUM	ACCT_KEY	MNTH_ID	DEBIT	CREDIT
16	16	202402	1600.00	
17	1	202402		340.27
18	15	202402		51.23
19	2	202402	51.23	
20	3	202402	11450.00	
21	14	202402		25800.00
22	8	202402		317.95
23	18	202402	317.95	
24	17	202402	12500.00	
25	9	202402		
26	10	202402		
27	11	202402	500.00	
28	21	202402	77.77	
29	22	202402	12.50	

June 2023

1. The premises rent of £1,600.00 is paid by bank card on June 2, reference PR-3.
2. The Savings account earns interest of £51.23 on June 6, reference 1024.
3. A bank card payment of £93.50 to settle the water bill on June 8, reference 1091
4. A bank card payment of £133.45 for Gas and Electricity is made on June 9, reference 611P.
5. On June 10, a consultancy invoice of £14,700.00 is generated and emailed to M&M, reference 773.
6. A payment of £10,500.00 is received from M&M on June 11, reference 514.
7. A payment of £8,450 is received from Witty Computer Systems on June 19, reference 882.
8. The month's payroll is run on June 23. The gross pay is £12,500.00; the calculated income tax is £4,500, and the net pay is £8,000. Reference: 06/24.
9. On June 24, June 24, the income tax of £ 4,500 was paid out, reference 06/24.
10. On the same day, the total net pay of £ 8,000 is paid out, reference 06/24.
11. On June 28, a water bill of £98.50 is received, reference 1091.
12. An Electricity and Gas Bill for £144.50 is received on June 30, reference 612.
13. On June 30, a long-term loan payment of £577.77 is made by direct bank debit, representing £500.00 principal and £77.77 loan interest, reference LTP-3.
14. Bank charges of £12.50 were collected from the checking account on June 30, reference BC-2.

The LEDGER listing below shows changes to account balances for the month:

ROW_NUM	ACCT_KEY	MNTH_ID	DEBIT	CREDIT
30	16	202403	1600.00	
31	1	202403	4032.78	
32	15	202403		51.23
33	2	202403	51.23	
34	8	202403		16.05
35	3	202403		4250.00
36	14	202403		14700.00
37	17	202403	12500.00	
38	9	202403		
39	10	202403		
40	18	202403	243.00	
41	11	202403	500.00	
42	21	202403	77.77	
43	22	202403	12.50	

July 2023

1. The premises rent of £1,600.00 is paid by bank card on July 2, reference PR-4.
2. The Savings account earns interest of £51.22 on July 6, reference 1025.
3. A bank card payment of £98.50 to settle the water bill on July 8, reference 1092
4. A bank card payment of £144.50 for Gas and Electricity is made on July 9, reference 611P.
5. On July 10, the owner withdraws £1,500 from the business checking account for personal use, reference CW-1.
6. On July 12, a consultancy invoice of £16,700.00 is generated and emailed to M&M, reference 774.
7. A payment of £10,500.00 is received from M&M on July 13, reference 515.
8. The month's payroll is run on July 23. The gross pay is £12,500.00; the calculated income tax is £4,500, and the net pay is £8,000. Reference: 07/24.
9. On July 24, the income tax of £ 4,500 was paid out, reference 07/24.
10. On the same day, July 24, the total net pay of £8,000 is paid out, reference 07/24.
11. On July 28, a water bill of £98.50 is received, reference 1092.
12. An Electricity and Gas Bill for £144.50 is received on July 30, reference 613.

13. On July 31, a long-term loan payment of £577.77 is made by direct bank debit, representing £500.00 principal and £77.77 loan interest, reference LTP-4.

14. Bank charges of £12.50 were collected from the checking account on July 31, reference BC-3.

The LEDGER listing below shows changes to the balances of the affected accounts:

ROW_NUM	ACCT_KEY	MNTH_ID	DEBIT	CREDIT
44	16	202404	1600.00	
45	1	202404		5933.27
46	15	202404		51.22
47	2	202404	51.22	
48	8	202404		
49	23	202404	1500.00	
50	3	202404	6200.00	
51	14	202404		16700.00
52	17	202404	12500.00	
53	9	202404		
54	10	202404		
55	18	202404	243.00	
56	11	202404	500.00	
57	21	202404	77.77	
58	22	202404	12.50	

August 2023

1. The premises rent of £1,600.00 is paid by bank card on August 2, reference PR-5.

2. The Savings account earns interest of £51.22 on August 6, reference 1026.

3. A bank card payment of £102.00 to settle the water bill on August 8, reference 1093

4. A bank card payment of £164.99 for Gas and Electricity is made on August 9, reference 612P.

5. On August 12, a consultancy invoice of £17,300.00 is generated and emailed to M&M, reference 775.

6. On August 13, a consultancy invoice of £18,200.00 is generated and emailed to Witty Computer Systems, reference 776.

7. A payment of £11,200.00 is received from M&M on August 15, reference 516.

8. On August 15, a year-end consultancy invoice of £18,200.00 is generated and emailed to Witty Computer Systems, reference 776-Y.

9. The bank approved a mortgage bond loan of £80,000 for the land they wish to build offices on August 16, reference ML-1.
10. The month's payroll is run on August 23. The gross pay is £12,500.00; the calculated income tax is £4,500, and the net pay is £8,000. Reference: 08/24.
11. On August 24, the total net pay of £ 8,000 is paid out, reference 08/24.
12. On the same day, August 24, the Income tax of £4,500 is paid out, reference 08/24.
13. On August 28, a water bill of £103.00 is received, reference 1093.
14. An Electricity and Gas Bill for £166.50 is received on August 30, reference 614.
15. On August 31, a long-term loan payment of £577.77 is made by direct bank debit, representing £500.00 principal and £77.77 loan interest, reference LTP-5.
16. Bank charges of £12.50 were collected from the checking account on August 31, reference BC-4.

The LEDGER listing below shows changes to the balances of the affected accounts:

ROW_NUM	ACCT_KEY	MNTH_ID	DEBIT	CREDIT
59	16	202405	1600.00	
60	1	202405		3757.26
61	15	202405		51.22
62	2	202405	51.22	
63	8	202405		2.51
64	3	202405	42500.00	
65	14	202405		53700.00
66	12	202405		80000.00
67	7	202405	80000.00	
68	17	202405	12500.00	
69	9	202405		
70	10	202405		
71	18	202405	269.50	
72	11	202405	500.00	
73	21	202405	77.77	
74	22	202405	12.50	

September 2023

1. The premises rent of £1,600.00 is paid by bank card on September 2, reference PR-6.

2. The Savings account earns interest of £51.22 on September 6, reference 1027.
3. A bank card payment of £103.00 to settle the water bill on September 8, reference 1093
4. A bank card payment of £166.50 for Gas and Electricity is made on September 9, reference 613P.
5. A consultancy invoice of £10,500 is generated and emailed to Witty Computer Systems on September 11, reference 518.
6. On September 12, a car is bought for £6,500 for business use, reference VP-1.
7. On September 13, a consultancy invoice of £18,200.00 is generated and emailed to Witty Computer Systems, reference 777.
8. On September 16, the bank collects the mortgage bond payment of £1,565, representing £462.00 interest and £1,103.00 principal, reference MP-1.
9. The month's payroll is run on September 23. The gross pay is £12,500.00; the calculated income tax is £4,500, and the net pay is £8,000. Reference: 09/24.
10. On September 24, the total net pay of £ 8,000 is paid out, reference 09/24.
11. On the same day, September 24, the Income tax of £4,500 is paid out, reference 09/24.
12. On September 28, a water bill of £103.00 is received, reference 1094.
13. An Electricity and Gas Bill for £166.50 is received on September 30, reference 615.
14. On September 30, a long-term loan payment of £577.77 is made by direct bank debit, representing £500.00 principal and £77.77 loan interest, reference LTP-6.
15. Bank charges of £12.50 were collected from the checking account on September 30, reference BC-5.
16. £16,000 is received from M&M on September 30, reference 518-2.

The LEDGER listing below shows changes to the balances of affected accounts:

ROW_NUM	ACCT_KEY	MNTH_ID	DEBIT	CREDIT
75	16	202406	1600.00	
76	1	202406		7024.77
77	15	202406		51.22
78	2	202406	51.22	
79	8	202406		
80	3	202406	12700.00	
81	14	202406		28700.00
82	6	202406	6500.00	
83	12	202406	1103.00	
84	21	202406	539.77	
85	17	202406	12500.00	
86	9	202406		
87	10	202406		
88	18	202406	269.50	
89	11	202406	500.00	
90	22	202406	12.50	

October 2023

1. The premises rent of £1,600.00 is paid by bank card on October 2, reference PR-7.
2. The Savings account earns interest of £51.22 on October 6, reference 1028.
3. A bank card payment of £103.00 to settle the water bill on October 8, reference 1094.
4. A bank card payment of £166.50 for Gas and Electricity is made on October 9, reference 614P.
5. £8,000 is received from M&M on October 11, reference 519.
6. On October 14, a consultancy invoice of £18,200.00 is generated and emailed to Witty Computer Systems, reference 778.
7. On October 16, the bank collects the mortgage bond payment of £1,565, representing £462.50 interest and £1,102.50 principal, reference MP-2.
8. The month's payroll is run on October 23. The gross pay is £12,500.00; the calculated income tax is £ 4,500.00, and the net pay is £ 8,000.00, reference 10/24.
9. On October 24, the total net pay of £8,000 is paid out, reference 10/24.
10. On the same day, October 24, the Income tax of £4,500 is paid out, reference 10/24.
11. On October 28, a water bill of £103.00 is received, reference 1095.

12. An Electricity and Gas Bill for £166.50 is received on October 31, reference 616.
13. On October 31, a long-term loan payment of £577.77 is made by direct bank debit, representing £500.00 principal and £77.77 loan interest, reference LTP-7.
14. Bank charges of £12.50 were collected from the checking account on October 31, reference BC-6.
15. On October 31, Witty Computer Systems transfers £18,500.00 into the business checking account, reference 519-2.

Changes to the balances of the affected accounts are depicted in the LEDGER entries below:

ROW_NUM	ACCT_KEY	MNTH_ID	DEBIT	CREDIT
91	16	202407	1600.00	
92	1	202407	9975.23	
93	15	202407		51.22
94	2	202407	51.22	
95	8	202407		
96	3	202407		8300.00
97	14	202407		18200.00
98	12	202407	1102.50	
99	21	202407	540.27	
100	17	202407	12500.00	
101	9	202407		
102	10	202407		
103	18	202407	269.50	
104	11	202407	500.00	
105	22	202407	12.50	

November 2023

1. The premises rent of £1,600.00 is paid by bank card on November 2, reference PR-8.
2. The Savings account earns interest of £51.22 on November 6, reference 1029.
3. A bank card payment of £103.00 to settle the water bill on November 8, reference 1095.
4. A bank card payment of £166.50 for Gas and Electricity is made on November 9, reference 615P.
5. £65.00 fuel is paid by bank card on November 11, reference 3356.
6. £16,200 is received from Witty Computer Systems on November 12, reference 520.

7. On November 15, consultancy invoices of £15,500.00 is generated and emailed to M&M, reference 779.
8. On November 16, the bank collects the mortgage bond payment of £1,565, representing £462.75 interest and £1,102.25 principal, reference MP-3.
9. The month's payroll is run on November 23. The gross pay is £12,500.00; the calculated income tax is £4,500, and the net pay is £8,000. Reference: 11/24.
10. On November 24, the total net pay of £ 8,000 is paid out, reference 11/24.
11. On the same day, November 24, the Income tax of £4,500 is paid out, reference 11/24.
12. On November 28, a water bill of £103.00 is received, reference 1096.
13. An Electricity and Gas Bill for £166.50 is received on November 30, reference 617.
14. On November 30, a long-term loan payment of £577.77 is made by direct bank debit, representing £500.00 principal and £77.77 loan interest, reference LTP-8.
15. Bank charges of £12.50 were collected from the checking account on November 30, reference BC-7.

The LEDGER changes to the balances of the affected accounts are listed below:

ROW_NUM	ACCT_KEY	MNTH_ID	DEBIT	CREDIT
106	16	202408	1600.00	
107	1	202408		389.77
108	15	202408		51.22
109	2	202408	51.22	
110	8	202408		
111	19	202408	65.00	
112	3	202408		700.00
113	14	202408		15500.00
114	12	202408	1102.25	
115	21	202408	540.52	
116	17	202408	12500.00	
117	9	202408		
118	10	202408		
119	18	202408	269.50	
120	11	202408	500.00	
121	22	202408	12.50	

December 2023

1. The premises rent of £1,600.00 is paid by bank card on December 2, reference PR-9.
2. The Savings account earns interest of £51.22 on December 6, reference 1030.
3. A bank card payment of £103.00 to settle the water bill on December 8, reference 1096.
4. A bank card payment of £166.50 for Gas and Electricity is made on December 9, reference 616P.
5. On December 11, a consultancy invoice of £12,500.00 is generated and emailed to M&M, reference 780.
6. On December 16, the bank collects the mortgage bond payment of £1,565, representing £462.75 interest and £1,102.25 principal, reference MP-4.
7. £53.00 fuel is paid by bank card on December 22, reference 3355.
8. The month's payroll is run on December 23. The gross pay is £12,500.00; the calculated income tax is £4,500, and the net pay is £8,000. Reference 12/24.
9. On December 24, the total net pay of £ 8,000 is paid out, reference 12/24.
10. On the same day, December 24, the Income tax of £4,500 is paid out, reference 12/24.
11. £12,500 is received from Witty Computer Systems on December 27, reference 522.
12. On December 28, a water bill of £103.00 is received, reference 1097.
13. An Electricity and Gas Bill for £166.50 is received on December 30, reference 618.
14. On December 31, a long-term loan payment of £577.77 is made by direct bank debit, representing £500.00 principal and £77.77 loan interest, reference LTP-9.
15. Bank charges of £12.50 were collected from the checking account on December 31, reference BC-8.

The LEDGER listing below shows changes to the balances of affected accounts:

ROW_NUM	ACCT_KEY	MNTH_ID	DEBIT	CREDIT
122	16	202409	1600.00	
123	1	202409		4077.77
124	15	202409		51.22
125	2	202409	51.22	
126	8	202409		
127	3	202409		
128	14	202409	0.00	12500.00
129	12	202409	1102.25	
130	21	202409	540.52	
131	19	202409	53.00	
132	17	202409	12500.00	
133	9	202409		
134	10	202409		
135	18	202409	269.50	
136	11	202409	500.00	
137	22	202409	12.50	

January 2024

1. The premises rent of £1,600.00 is paid by direct debit on January 2, reference DD-1.
2. The Savings account earns interest of £51.22 on January 6, reference 1031.
3. A bank card payment of £103.00 to settle the water bill on January 8, reference 1097.
4. A bank card payment of £166.50 for Gas and Electricity is made on January 9, reference 617P.
5. £53.00 fuel is paid by bank card on January 10, reference 3358.
6. £14,500 is received from Witty Computer Systems on January 10, reference 523.
7. On January 11, a consultancy invoice of £18,500.00 is generated and emailed to M&M, reference 781.
8. On January 16, the bank collects the mortgage bond payment of £1,565, representing £462.75 interest and £1,102.25 principal, reference MP-5.
9. The month's payroll is run on January 23. The gross pay is £12,500.00; the calculated income tax is £4,500, and the net pay is £8,000. Reference: 01/25.
10. On January 24, the total net pay of £ 8,000 is paid out, reference 01/25.
11. On the same day, January 24, the Income tax of £4,500 is paid out, reference 01/25.

12. £8,500 is received from M&M on January 27, reference 524.
13. On January 28, a water bill of £103.00 is received, reference 1098.
14. An Electricity and Gas Bill for £166.50 is received on January 30, reference 619.
15. On January 31, a long-term loan payment of £577.77 is made by direct bank debit, representing £500.00 principal and £77.77 loan interest, reference LTP-10.
16. Bank charges of £12.50 were collected from the checking account on January 31, reference BC-9.

The LEDGER changes to the balances of the affected accounts are listed below:

ROW_NUM	ACCT_KEY	MNTH_ID	DEBIT	CREDIT
138	16	202410	1600.00	
139	1	202410	6422.23	
140	15	202410		51.22
141	2	202410	51.22	
142	8	202410		
143	19	202410	53.00	
144	3	202410		4500.00
145	14	202410		18500.00
146	12	202410	1102.25	
147	21	202410	540.52	
148	17	202410	12500.00	
149	9	202410		
150	10	202410		
151	18	202410	269.50	
152	11	202410	500.00	
153	22	202410	12.50	

February 2024

1. The premises rent of £1,600.00 is paid by direct debit on February 2, reference DD-2.
2. The Savings account earns interest of £51.22 on February 6, reference 1032.
3. A bank card payment of £103.00 to settle the water bill on February 8, reference 1098.
4. A bank card payment of £166.50 for Gas and Electricity is made on February 9, reference 618P.
5. £120.00 train tickets to a client are paid for by bank card on February 10, reference 3359.

6. £15,500 is received from M&M on February 10, reference 524.
7. On February 11, a consultancy invoice of £18,500.00 is generated and emailed to M&M, reference 782.
8. On February 16, the bank collects the mortgage bond payment of £1,565, representing £462.75 interest and £1,102.25 principal, reference MP-6.
9. The month's payroll is run on February 23. The gross pay is £12,500.00; the calculated income tax is £4,500, and the net pay is £8,000, reference 02/25.
10. On February 24, the total net pay of £ 8,000 is paid out, reference 02/25.
11. On the same day, February 24, the Income tax of £4 500 is paid out, reference 02/25.
12. £10,500 is received from Witty Computer Systems on February 26, reference 525.
13. On February 27, a water bill of £103.00 is received, reference 1099.
14. An Electricity and Gas Bill for £166.50 is received on February 27, reference 620.
15. On February 28, a long-term loan payment of £577.77 is made by direct bank debit, representing £500.00 principal and £77.77 loan interest, reference LTP-11.
16. Bank charges of £12.50 were collected from the checking account on February 28, reference BC-10.

The changes to balances of the affected accounts are listed below:

ROW_NUM	ACCT_KEY	MNTH_ID	DEBIT	CREDIT
154	16	202411	1600.00	
155	1	202411	9355.23	
156	15	202411		51.22
157	2	202411	51.22	
158	8	202411		
159	19	202411	120.00	
160	3	202411		7500.00
161	14	202411		18500.00
162	12	202411	1102.25	
163	21	202411	540.52	
164	17	202411	12500.00	
165	9	202411		
166	10	202411		
167	18	202411	269.50	
168	11	202411	500.00	
169	22	202411	12.50	

March 2024

1. The premises rent of £1,600.00 is paid by direct debit on March 2, reference DD-3.
2. The Savings account earns interest of £51.22 on March 6, reference 1033.
3. A bank card payment of £103.00 to settle the water bill on March 8, reference 1099.
4. A bank card payment of £166.50 for Gas and Electricity is made on March 9, reference 619P.
5. £35.50 fuel is paid by bank card on March 10, reference 3360.
6. £12,200 is received from Witty Computer Systems on March 10, reference 525.
7. On March 12, a consultancy invoice of £21,750.00 is generated and emailed to DZK Limited, reference 783.
8. On March 13, a consultancy invoice of £11,500.00 is generated and emailed to M&M, reference 784.
9. On March 16, the bank collects the mortgage bond payment of £1,565, representing £462.75 interest and £1,102.25 principal, reference MP-8.
10. The month's payroll is run on March 23. The gross pay is £12,500.00; the calculated income tax is £4,500, and the net pay is £8,000. Reference: 03/25.
11. On March 24, the total net pay of £ 8,000 is paid out, reference 03/25.
12. On the same day, March 24, the Income tax of £4,500 is paid out, reference 03/25.
13. £11,250 is received from Witty Computer Systems on March 26, reference 526.
14. On March 27, a water bill of £103.00 is received, reference 1100.
15. An Electricity and Gas Bill for £166.50 is received on March 27, reference 621.
16. On March 30, a long-term loan payment of £577.77 is made by direct bank debit, representing £500.00 principal and £77.77 loan interest, reference LTP-12.
17. Bank charges of £12.50 were collected from the checking account on March 31, reference BC-11.
18. The owner withdraws £3,500 from the business checking account for personal use on March 31, reference CW-2.

The LEDGER listing below shows the changes to the balances of the affected accounts:

ROW_NUM	ACCT_KEY	MNTH_ID	DEBIT	CREDIT
170	16	202412	1600.00	
171	1	202412	3389.73	
172	15	202412		51.22
173	2	202412	51.22	
174	8	202412		
175	19	202412	35.50	
176	3	202412	9800.00	
177	14	202412		33250.00
178	12	202412	1102.25	
179	21	202412	540.52	
180	17	202412	12500.00	
181	9	202412		
182	10	202412		
183	18	202412	269.50	
184	11	202412	500.00	
185	22	202412	12.50	
186	23	202412	3500.00	

CHAPTER 12

Year-end Process

The year-end process marks the end of an accounting year. A simplified year-end process encompasses the following:

- Preparation of financial statements for the year
- Transfer of balances from temporary accounts to the capital account
- Carry forward of balances of permanent accounts to the opening month of the following year
- Opening of the first month of the new year for processing

If you have processed all the transactions in the last chapter, the LEDGER table should have 186 rows, and the account balances should be as shown in the Trial Balance sample below:

Number	Account	Debit	Credit
	Murewa Consultancy		
	Trial Balance		
	March 31, 2024		
1000	Checking account	£25,764.32	
1010	Savings account	5,563.44	
1020	Accounts receivable	67,250.00	
1500	Office furniture	4,560.00	
1510	Computer hardware	11,400.00	
1520	Vehicles	6,500.00	
1530	Land and property	80,000.00	
2000	Accounts payable		£437.51
2500	Long-term loan		24,000.00
2510	Mortgage loan		72,283.25
3000	Capital		15,000.00
4000	Consultancy Revenue		270,650.00
4010	Interest earned		563.44
5000	Office rent	19,200.00	
5010	Staff salaries	150,000.00	
5020	Utilities	3,060.95	
5030	Travel	326.50	
5040	Loan Interest	4,171.49	
5050	Bank Charges	137.50	
6000	Drawings	5,000.00	
Totals		**£382,934.20**	**£382,934.20**

Annual results

Financial statements present annual results to the owner, investors, lenders, and other interested parties.

Income Statement

The income statement, the most reviewed financial statement, may be comparative. It compares the performance of the business between the current year and the previous year, as illustrated in the sample below:

	Murewa Consultancy Income Statement for year ending March 31, 2024			
	Year 2023	Year 2024	Absolute Change	% Change
Revenues				
Consultancy Revenue		270,650.00	270,650.00	
Interest earned		563.44	563.44	
Total Revenues		271,213.44	271,213.44	
Expenses				
Office rent		19,200.00	19,200.00	
Gross Pay		150,000.00	150,000.00	
Utilities		3,060.95	3,060.95	
Travel		326.50	326.50	
Loan Interest		4,171.49	4,171.49	
Bank Charges		137.50	137.50	
Total Expenses		176,896.44	176,896.44	
Net Income (Profit/Loss)		94,317.00	94,317.00	

The following T-SQL query extracts the data used as input for preparing the year-end comparative financial statement:

```
DECLARE      @MNTH_ID          INT = 202412

SELECT
      AE.ELEMENT, A.ACCT_ID, A.ACCT_NAME,
      SUM(CASE WHEN
               L.MNTH_ID BETWEEN @MNTH_ID - 111 AND
@MNTH_ID - 100 THEN
               CASE WHEN AE.SIDE = 'Debit' THEN
                  ISNULL(L.DEBIT, 0) - ISNULL(L.CREDIT, 0)
ELSE
                  ISNULL(L.CREDIT, 0) - ISNULL(L.DEBIT, 0)
            END
```

```
                END) AS PREV_YEAR,
        SUM(CASE WHEN
                    L.MNTH_ID BETWEEN @MNTH_ID - 11 AND
@MNTH_ID THEN
                    CASE WHEN
                    AE.SIDE = 'Debit' THEN
                    ISNULL(L.DEBIT, 0) - ISNULL(L.CREDIT, 0) ELSE
                    ISNULL(L.CREDIT, 0) - ISNULL(L.DEBIT, 0) END
                END ) AS CURRENT_YEAR
FROM
        ACCOUNTING_EQUATION AS AE
JOIN
        ACCOUNT AS A
        ON      AE.ELEMENT_ID = A.ELEMENT_ID
JOIN
        LEDGER AS L
        ON      A.ACCT_KEY = L.ACCT_KEY
WHERE
        AE.ELEMENT IN ('Revenue', 'Expenses') AND
        L.MNTH_ID BETWEEN @MNTH_ID - 111 AND @MNTH_ID
GROUP BY
        AE.ELEMENT, A.ACCT_ID, A.ACCT_NAME
ORDER BY
        A.ACCT_ID
```

The following resultset has enough data to generate the year-end comparative income statement:

ELEMENT	ACCT_ID	ACCT_NAME	PREV_YEAR	CURRENT_YEAR
Revenue	4000	Consultancy Revenue		270650.00
Revenue	4010	Interest earned		563.44
Expenses	5000	Office rent		19200.00
Expenses	5010	Staff salaries		150000.00
Expenses	5020	Utilities		3060.95
Expenses	5030	Travel		326.50
Expenses	5040	Loan Interest		4171.49
Expenses	5050	Bank Charges		137.50

Balance Sheet

A comparative balance sheet that compares the financial position of the business between the current year and the previous year may be produced, as illustrated in the sample below:

Murewa Consultancy Balance Sheet for year ending March 31, 2024		
Assets	Year 2024	Year 2023
Current Assets		
Checking account	25,764.32	-
Savings account	5,563.44	-
Accounts receivable	67,250.00	-
Total Current Assets	**98,577.76**	
Long-term Assets		
Office furniture	4,560.00	-
Computer hardware	11,400.00	-
Vehicles	6,500.00	-
Land and property	80,000.00	-
Total Long-term Assets	**102,460.00**	**-**
Total Assets	**201,037.76**	**-**
Liabilities		
Current Liabilities		
Accounts payable	437.51	-
Total Current Liabilities	**437.51**	**-**
Long-term Liabilities		
Long-term loan	24,000.00	-
Mortgage loan	72,283.25	-
Long-term Liabilities	**96,283.25**	**-**
Owner's Equity		
Capital	15,000.00	-
Net Income (Profit/Loss)	94,317.00	-
Drawings	-5,000.00	-
	104,317.00	**-**
Total Liabilities and Owner's Equity	**201,037.76**	**-**

The following T-SQL query extracts the data used as input for preparing the year-end comparative financial statement:

```
DECLARE @MNTH_ID          INT = 202412

SELECT
      AE.ELEMENT, CASE WHEN AE.ELEMENT = 'Owner''s Equity' THEN
AE.ELEMENT ELSE CT.CATEGORY END AS CATEGORY,
      CASE WHEN CATEGORY = 'Net Income (Profit/Loss)' THEN 4000
ELSE A.ACCT_ID END AS ACCT_ID,
      CASE WHEN CATEGORY = 'Net Income (Profit/Loss)' THEN CAT-
EGORY ELSE A.ACCT_NAME END AS ACCT_NAME,
      SUM(
      CASE WHEN L.MNTH_ID BETWEEN ROUND(@MNTH_ID, -2)
AND @MNTH_ID THEN
            CASE WHEN AE.SIDE = 'Debit' THEN ISNULL(L.DEBIT, 0) -
ISNULL(L.CREDIT, 0) ELSE
```

```
                    ISNULL(L.CREDIT, 0) - ISNULL(L.DEBIT, 0)
            END
     END
     ) AS CURRENT_YEAR,
     SUM(
     CASE WHEN L.MNTH_ID BETWEEN ROUND(@MNTH_ID - 100, -
2) AND @MNTH_ID - 100 THEN
            CASE WHEN AE.SIDE = 'Debit' THEN ISNULL(L.DEBIT, 0) -
ISNULL(L.CREDIT, 0) ELSE
                    ISNULL(L.CREDIT, 0) - ISNULL(L.DEBIT, 0)
            END
     END
     ) AS PREV_YEAR
FROM
     ACCOUNTING_EQUATION AS AE
JOIN
     BS_CATEGORY AS CT
     ON     AE.ELEMENT_ID = CT.ELEMENT_ID
JOIN
     ACCOUNT AS A
     ON     A.CATEGORY_ID = CT.CATEGORY_ID
JOIN
     LEDGER AS L
     ON     A.ACCT_KEY = L.ACCT_KEY
WHERE
     L.MNTH_ID BETWEEN ROUND(@MNTH_ID -100, -2) AND
@MNTH_ID
GROUP BY
     AE.ELEMENT,
     CASE WHEN AE.ELEMENT = 'Owner''s Equity' THEN AE.ELEMENT
ELSE CT.CATEGORY END,
     CASE WHEN CT.CATEGORY = 'Net Income (Profit/Loss)' THEN
4000 ELSE A.ACCT_ID END,
     CASE WHEN CT.CATEGORY = 'Net Income (Profit/Loss)' THEN
CT.CATEGORY ELSE A.ACCT_NAME END
HAVING
     SUM(
     CASE WHEN L.MNTH_ID BETWEEN ROUND(@MNTH_ID, -2)
AND @MNTH_ID THEN
            CASE WHEN AE.SIDE = 'Debit' THEN ISNULL(L.DEBIT, 0) -
ISNULL(L.CREDIT, 0) ELSE
                    ISNULL(L.CREDIT, 0) - ISNULL(L.DEBIT, 0)
            END
     END
     ) <> 0.00 OR
     SUM(
```

```
        CASE WHEN L.MNTH_ID BETWEEN ROUND(@MNTH_ID - 100, -
2) AND @MNTH_ID - 100 THEN
            CASE WHEN AE.SIDE = 'Debit' THEN ISNULL(L.DEBIT, 0) -
ISNULL(L.CREDIT, 0) ELSE
                ISNULL(L.CREDIT, 0) - ISNULL(L.DEBIT, 0)
        END
    END
    ) <> 0.00
ORDER BY
    3
```

The query produces the following resultset:

ELEMENT	BS_HEADING	ACCT_ID	ACCT_NAME	CURR_YEAR	PREV_YEAR
Assets	Current Assets	1000	Checking account	25764.32	
Assets	Current Assets	1010	Savings account	5563.44	
Assets	Current Assets	1020	Accounts Receivable	67250.00	
Assets	Long-term Assets	1500	Office furniture	4560.00	
Assets	Long-term Assets	1510	Computer Hardware	11400.00	
Assets	Long-term Assets	1520	Vehicles	6500.00	
Assets	Long-term Assets	1530	Land and property	80000.00	
Liabilities	Current Liabilities	2000	Accounts payable	437.51	
Liabilities	Long-term Liabilities	2500	Long-term loan	24000.00	
Liabilities	Long-term Liabilities	2510	Mortgage loan	72283.25	
Owner's Equity	Owner's Equity	3000	Capital	15000.00	
Owner's Equity	Owner's Equity	4000	Net Income (Profit/Loss)	94317.00	
Owner's Equity	Owner's Equity	6000	Drawings	-5000.00	

Cash Flow Statement

The year-end provides an opportunity to prepare a comparative cash flow statement that shows two or more consecutive years.

The report may be used, among other things, to assess how much cash is spent chasing revenues from one month to the next and how cash movements vary over time.

Murewa Consultancy Statement of Cash Flows for year ending March 31, 2024		
	Year 2024	Year 2023
Operating Activities		
Cash received from customers	203,400.00	
Interest Received	563.44	
Cash paid to Employees	-96,000.00	
Cash paid for Income Tax	-54,000.00	
Cash paid for other operating expenses	-22,287.44	
Net cash from Operating Activities [A]	**31,676.00**	
Investing Activities		
Purchase of property and equipment	-22,460.00	
Sale of property and equipment	0.00	
Net cash from Investing Activities [B]	**-22,460.00**	
Financing Activities		
Add: Investment by the owner	15,000.00	
Add: long-term debt	30,000.00	
Less: Repayments of long-term debt	-17,888.24	
Less: Withdrawals by the owner	-5,000.00	
Net cash from Financing Activities [C]	**22,111.76**	
Net Increase/Decrease in Cash (A+B+C)	**31,327.76**	
Opening Cash Balance	0.00	
Ending Cash Balance	**31,327.76**	

The following T-SQL query extracts the data used as input for preparing the year-end comparative financial statement:

```
DECLARE      @MNTH_ID           INT = 202412;
WITH OB AS
(
SELECT
      4 AS ACTIVITY_ID, 'Opening Cash Balance' AS ACTIVITY,
      99 AS CF_ID,
      '' AS CATEGORY,
      ISNULL(SUM(CASE WHEN L.MNTH_ID = ROUND(@MNTH_ID, -
2) THEN
            ISNULL(L.DEBIT, 0) - ISNULL(L.CREDIT, 0) END), 0) AS
AMOUNT,
      ISNULL(SUM(CASE WHEN L.MNTH_ID = ROUND(@MNTH_ID -
100, -2) THEN
            ISNULL(L.DEBIT, 0) - ISNULL(L.CREDIT, 0) END), 0) AS
PY_AMOUNT
FROM
      LEDGER AS L
JOIN
      ACCOUNT AS A
```

```
        ON      L.ACCT_KEY = A.ACCT_KEY
WHERE
        A.CCE_IND = 1 AND
        (
        L.MNTH_ID = ROUND(@MNTH_ID, -2) OR
        L.MNTH_ID = ROUND(@MNTH_ID - 100, -2)
        )
)
SELECT
        A.ACTIVITY_ID, A.ACTIVITY + ' Activities' AS ACTIVITY,
        H.CF_ID,
        H.CATEGORY,
        ISNULL(SUM(CASE WHEN J.MNTH_ID BETWEEN
ROUND(@MNTH_ID, -2) + 1 AND @MNTH_ID THEN
                ISNULL(J.DEBIT, 0) - ISNULL(J.CREDIT, 0) END), 0) AS
AMOUNT,
        ISNULL(SUM(CASE WHEN J.MNTH_ID BETWEEN
ROUND(@MNTH_ID - 100, -2) + 1 AND ROUND(@MNTH_ID - 100, -2) +
12 THEN
                ISNULL(J.DEBIT, 0) - ISNULL(J.CREDIT, 0) END), 0) AS
PY_AMOUNT
FROM
        ACTIVITY AS A
JOIN
        CF_CATEGORY AS H
        ON      A.ACTIVITY_ID = H.ACTIVITY_ID
LEFT JOIN
        JOURNAL AS J
        ON      H.CF_ID = J.CF_ID AND
        (
                J.MNTH_ID BETWEEN ROUND(@MNTH_ID, -2) + 1 AND
@MNTH_ID OR
                J.MNTH_ID BETWEEN ROUND(@MNTH_ID - 100, -2) + 1
AND ROUND(@MNTH_ID - 100, -2) + 12 )
GROUP BY
        A.ACTIVITY_ID, A.ACTIVITY + ' Activities',
        H.CF_ID,
        H.CATEGORY
UNION ALL
SELECT
        ACTIVITY_ID, ACTIVITY, CF_ID, CATEGORY, AMOUNT,
PY_AMOUNT
FROM
        OB
ORDER BY
        ACTIVITY_ID, CF_ID
```

The following resultset has both the current and previous year figures:

ACTIVITY_ID	ACTIVITY	CF_ID	CF_HEADING	CASH	PY_CASH
1	Operating Activities	1	Cash received from customers	203400.00	
1	Operating Activities	2	Interest received	563.44	
1	Operating Activities	3	Cash paid to Employees	-96000.00	
1	Operating Activities	4	Cash paid for Income Tax	-54000.00	
1	Operating Activities	5	Cash paid for other operating expenses	-22287.44	
2	Investing Activities	6	Purchase of property and equipment	-22460.00	
2	Investing Activities	7	Sale of property and equipment	0.00	
3	Financing Activities	8	Add: Investment by the owner	15000.00	
3	Financing Activities	9	Add: long-term debt	30000.00	
3	Financing Activities	10	Less: Repayments of long-term debt	-17888.24	
3	Financing Activities	11	Less: Withdrawals by the owner	-5000.00	
4	Opening Cash Balance	99		0.00	

Transfer of balances from temporary accounts

The extended accounting equation below is a reminder that revenue, expenses, and withdrawals are applied to the owner's equity after the fiscal year-end.

assets = liabilities + owner's equity + revenue – expenses - withdrawals

As indicated in Chapter 3, month 13 is used to record the transfer of balances from revenue, expenses, and withdrawal accounts to the capital account.

The balances of the nine temporary accounts in fiscal month 202412 are as follows:

ACCT_KEY	ACCT_ID	ACCT_NAME	DEBIT	CREDIT
14	4000	Consultancy revenue		270650.00
15	4010	Interest earned		563.44
16	5000	Office rent	19200.00	
17	5010	Staff salaries	150000.00	
18	5020	Utilities	3060.95	
19	5030	Travel	326.50	
21	5040	Loan Interest	4171.49	
22	5050	Bank Charges	137.50	
23	6000	Drawings	5000.00	

For each temporary account with a credit balance (e.g. Consultancy revenue), the following journal entries of the same amount are created:

Temporary account	Capital account
Debit journal entry	Credit journal entry

The following two journal entries are generated for each temporary account with a debit balance (e.g. Office rent):

Temporary account	Capital account
Credit journal entry	Debit journal entry

The overall effect on the Capital account is either a debit or credit of the difference between the total debits and total credits of temporary accounts. In this instance, the credit is £89,317.00.

The following T-SQL code, with a Fiscal Year parameter, generates the year-end journal entries and updates the LEDGER.

```
DECLARE    @YEAR           INT = 2024
DECLARE    @FROM         INT = @YEAR * 100 + 1
DECLARE    @TO            INT = @YEAR * 100 + 12
DECLARE    @MNTH_ID   INT = @YEAR * 100 + 13
DECLARE    @CAPITAL_ACCT    INT = (SELECT ACCT_KEY FROM AC-
COUNT WHERE ACCT_NAME = 'CAPITAL')
;
WITH BAL AS
(
     SELECT
```

```
            A.ACCT_KEY, ACCT_ID, A.ACCT_NAME, CASE WHEN
SUM(ISNULL(DEBIT, 0)) >=  SUM(ISNULL(CREDIT, 0)) THEN
                SUM(ISNULL(DEBIT, 0)) - SUM(ISNULL(CREDIT, 0))
ELSE 0 END AS DEBIT,
                CASE WHEN SUM(ISNULL(DEBIT, 0)) <=
SUM(ISNULL(CREDIT, 0)) THEN
                SUM(ISNULL(CREDIT, 0)) - SUM(ISNULL(DEBIT, 0))
ELSE 0 END AS CREDIT
      FROM
            ACCOUNT AS A
      JOIN
            ACCOUNTING_EQUATION AS AE
            ON      A.ELEMENT_ID = AE.ELEMENT_ID
      JOIN
            LEDGER AS L
            ON      A.ACCT_KEY = L.ACCT_KEY
      WHERE
            AE.ELEMENT_TYPE = 'TEMPORARY' AND
            L.MNTH_ID BETWEEN @FROM AND @TO
      GROUP BY
            A.ACCT_KEY, ACCT_ID, A.ACCT_NAME
)
INSERT
      JOURNAL
SELECT
      -@YEAR AS JRNL_NUM, @CAPITAL_ACCT AS ACCT_KEY, NULL
AS TRAN_DATE, NULL AS TRAN_REF,
      @MNTH_ID AS MNTH_ID, 'Transfer from temp accounts'
AS NARRATIVE,
      CASE WHEN SUM(DEBIT) >= SUM(CREDIT) THEN SUM(DEBIT) -
SUM(CREDIT) ELSE 0 END AS DEBIT,
      CASE WHEN SUM(DEBIT) <= SUM(CREDIT) THEN SUM(CREDIT)
- SUM(DEBIT) ELSE 0 END AS CREDIT,
      NULL AS CF_ID
FROM
      BAL
UNION ALL
SELECT
      -@YEAR AS JRNL_NUM, ACCT_KEY, NULL AS TRAN_DATE, NULL
AS TRAN_REF,
      @MNTH_ID AS MNTH_ID, 'Transfer to Capital' AS NARRATIVE,
      CASE WHEN CREDIT >= DEBIT THEN CREDIT - DEBIT ELSE 0 END
AS DEBIT,
      CASE WHEN DEBIT >= CREDIT THEN DEBIT - CREDIT ELSE 0 END
AS CREDIT,
      NULL AS CF_ID
FROM
```

```
        BAL
INSERT
        LEDGER
SELECT
        ACCT_KEY, MNTH_ID, DEBIT, CREDIT
FROM
        JOURNAL
WHERE
        MNTH_ID = @MNTH_ID
```

The year-end journal entries created are listed below:

JRNL_NUM	ACCT_KEY	MNTH_ID	NARRATIVE	DEBIT	CREDIT
-2024	13	202413	Transfer from temp accounts		89317.00
-2024	14	202413	Transfer to Capital	270650.00	
-2024	15	202413	Transfer to Capital	563.44	
-2024	16	202413	Transfer to Capital		19200.00
-2024	17	202413	Transfer to Capital		150000.00
-2024	18	202413	Transfer to Capital		3060.95
-2024	19	202413	Transfer to Capital		326.50
-2024	21	202413	Transfer to Capital		4171.49
-2024	22	202413	Transfer to Capital		137.50
-2024	23	202413	Transfer to Capital		5000.00

The negative journal number, denoting the financial year, differentiates it from the other journal entries. And the following entries are recorded in LEDGER table:

ROW_NUM	ACCT_KEY	MNTH_ID	DEBIT	CREDIT
187	13	202413		89317.00
188	14	202413	270650.00	
189	15	202413	563.44	
190	16	202413		19200.00
191	17	202413		150000.00
192	18	202413		3060.95
193	19	202413		326.50
194	21	202413		4171.49
195	22	202413		137.50
196	23	202413		5000.00

The transfer of balances from temporary accounts to the capital account signifies the closure of the fiscal year.

Post-closing Trial Balance

Below is the post-closing Trial Balance:

Murewa Consultancy				
Post-closing Trial Balance				
March 31, 2024				
Number	**Account**		**Debit**	**Credit**
1000	Checking account		£25,764.32	
1010	Savings account		5,563.44	
1020	Accounts receivable		67,250.00	
1500	Office furniture		4,560.00	
1510	Computer hardware		11,400.00	
1520	Vehicles		6,500.00	
1530	Land and property		80,000.00	
2000	Accounts payable			£437.51
2500	Long-term loan			24,000.00
2510	Mortgage loan			72,283.25
3000	Capital			104,317.00
Totals			**£201,037.76**	**£201,037.76**

Temporary accounts are not listed. Their balances have been transferred to the Capital account, as reflected in the new balance. The following T-SQL code, run for the period 202413, retrieves the post-closing account balances:

```
DECLARE    @MNTH_ID  INT = 202413

SELECT
      A.ACCT_ID,
      A.ACCT_NAME,
      SUM(CASE
        WHEN AE.SIDE = 'DEBIT'
      THEN
        ISNULL(L.DEBIT, 0) - ISNULL(L.CREDIT, 0) END) AS DEBIT,
      SUM(CASE
        WHEN AE.SIDE = 'CREDIT'
      THEN
        ISNULL(L.CREDIT, 0) - ISNULL(L.DEBIT, 0) END) AS CREDIT
FROM
      LEDGER AS L
JOIN
      ACCOUNT AS A
      ON    L.ACCT_KEY = A.ACCT_KEY
JOIN
      ACCOUNTING_EQUATION AS AE
```

```
        ON      A.ELEMENT_ID = AE.ELEMENT_ID
WHERE
        L.MNTH_ID BETWEEN ROUND(@MNTH_ID, -2) AND
@MNTH_ID
GROUP BY
        A.ACCT_ID,
        A.ACCT_NAME
HAVING
        SUM(CASE
            WHEN AE.SIDE = 'DEBIT'
            THEN
            ISNULL(L.DEBIT, 0) - ISNULL(L.CREDIT, 0) END) <> 0
        OR
        SUM(CASE
            WHEN AE.SIDE = 'CREDIT'
            THEN
            ISNULL(L.CREDIT, 0) - ISNULL(L.DEBIT, 0) END) <> 0
ORDER BY
A.ACCT_ID
```

Opening balances for the new year

The following code, which accepts the closed fiscal year as a parameter, loads opening balances for the following year into the LEDGER table:

```
DECLARE    @YEAR              INT = 2024
DECLARE    @FROM              INT = @YEAR * 100
DECLARE    @TO                INT = @YEAR * 100 + 13
DECLARE    @OPENING_MNTH  INT = (@YEAR + 1) * 100

INSERT
        LEDGER
SELECT
        A.ACCT_KEY, @OPENING_MNTH AS MNTH_ID,
        CASE WHEN SUM(ISNULL(DEBIT, 0)) >=  SUM(ISNULL(CREDIT,
0)) THEN
                SUM(ISNULL(DEBIT, 0)) - SUM(ISNULL(CREDIT, 0)) ELSE
NULL END AS DEBIT,
                CASE WHEN SUM(ISNULL(DEBIT, 0)) <=
SUM(ISNULL(CREDIT, 0)) THEN
                SUM(ISNULL(CREDIT, 0)) - SUM(ISNULL(DEBIT, 0)) ELSE
NULL END AS CREDIT
FROM
        ACCOUNT AS A
```

```
JOIN
        ACCOUNTING_EQUATION AS AE
        ON      A.ELEMENT_ID = AE.ELEMENT_ID
JOIN
        LEDGER AS L
        ON      A.ACCT_KEY = L.ACCT_KEY
WHERE
        L.MNTH_ID BETWEEN @FROM AND @TO
GROUP BY
        A.ACCT_KEY, ACCT_ID, A.ACCT_NAME
HAVING
        CASE WHEN SUM(ISNULL(DEBIT, 0)) >= SUM(ISNULL(CREDIT,
0)) THEN
                SUM(ISNULL(DEBIT, 0)) - SUM(ISNULL(CREDIT, 0)) ELSE
0 END <> 0 OR
        CASE WHEN SUM(ISNULL(DEBIT, 0)) <= SUM(ISNULL(CREDIT,
0)) THEN
                SUM(ISNULL(CREDIT, 0)) - SUM(ISNULL(DEBIT, 0)) ELSE
0 END <> 0
```

The following 11 accounts have their opening balances loaded in the period 202500:

ROW_NUM	ACCT_KEY	MNTH_ID	DEBIT	CREDIT
197	1	202500	25764.32	
198	2	202500	5563.44	
199	3	202500	67250.00	
200	4	202500	4560.00	
201	5	202500	11400.00	
202	6	202500	6500.00	
203	7	202500	80000.00	
204	8	202500		437.51
205	11	202500		24000.00
206	12	202500		72283.25
207	13	202500		104317.00

Opening the first month of the year in the FISCAL_MONTH table starts another annual accounting cycle, as shown below:

MNTH_ID	YEAR_ID	START_DATE	END_DATE	COMMENTS	MONTH_STATUS
202413	2024				
202500	2025				
202501	2025	01/04/2024	30/04/2024		OPEN

CHAPTER 13

Budgeting and cash-flow forecasting

The parts of the SOKO data model presented so far are backwards-looking. A comprehensive accounting system is also forward-looking, enabling budgeting and cash-flow forecasting.

Budgeting

Budget projections are estimates of revenue and expenses for every month of a fiscal year. The projections are typically based on historical financial data from all sources of revenue and types of expenses, and account for the unexpected.

The BUDGET table, described below, holds projected monthly revenue and expenses by account.

Column Name	Description	Type	Length	Null	Key	Foreign Table
ROW_NUM	Unique Id	bigint		N	P	
ACCT_KEY	Account key	Int		N	F	ACCOUNT
MNTH_ID	Month Id	Int		N	F	FISCAL_MONTH
DEBIT	Debit movement (If any)	money		Y		
CREDIT	Credit movement (if any)	money		Y		

The listing below provides an example of projected revenue and expenses for the first two months of Fiscal Year 2024:

ROW_NUM	ACCT_KEY	MNTH_ID	DEBIT	CREDIT
1	14	202401		31556.00
2	15	202401		77.00
3	16	202401	2080.00	
4	17	202401	16250.00	
5	18	202401	332.00	
6	19	202401	85.00	
7	20	202401	84.00	
8	21	202401	452.00	
9	22	202401	16.00	
10	14	202402		31556.00
11	15	202402		77.00
12	16	202402	2080.00	
13	17	202402	16250.00	
14	18	202402	332.00	
15	19	202402	85.00	
16	20	202402	84.00	
17	21	202402	452.00	
18	22	202402	16.00	

The Income Statement below, as of May 2023, compares actuals to budgets for the month and year-to-date:

	Murewa Consultancy **Income Statement** **for month ending May 31, 2023**					
	May-23			Year to Date		
	Actuals	Budget	Variance	Actuals	Budget	Variance
Revenues						
Consultancy Revenue	25,800.00	31,556.00	-5,756.00	40,400.00	63,112.00	-22,712.00
Interest earned	51.23	77.00	-25.77	51.23	154.00	-102.77
Total Revenues	25,851.23	31,633.00	-5,781.77	40,451.23	63,266.00	-22,814.77
Expenses						
Office rent	1,600.00	2,080.00	-480.00	3,200.00	4,160.00	-960.00
Staff salaries	12,500.00	16,250.00	-3,750.00	25,000.00	32,500.00	-7,500.00
Utilities	317.95	332.00	-14.05	418.95	664.00	-245.05
Travel	0.00	85.00	-85.00	0.00	170.00	-170.00
Office sundries	0.00	84.00	-84.00	0.00	168.00	-168.00
Loan Interest	77.77	452.00	-374.23	155.54	904.00	-748.46
Bank Charges	12.50	16.00	-3.50	12.50	32.00	-19.50
Total Expenses	14,508.22	19,299.00	-4,790.78	28,786.99	38,598.00	-9,811.01
Net Income (Loss)	11,343.01	12,334.00	-990.99	11,664.24	24,668.00	-13,003.76

The following is an example of T-SQL data retrieval code:

```
DECLARE      @MNTH_ID   INT = 202402;
WITH RSLT AS
(
SELECT
      AE.ELEMENT, A.ACCT_ID, A.ACCT_NAME,
      (CASE WHEN L.MNTH_ID = @MNTH_ID THEN
            CASE WHEN AE.SIDE = 'Debit' THEN
                  ISNULL(L.DEBIT, 0) - ISNULL(L.CREDIT, 0) ELSE
                  ISNULL(L.CREDIT, 0) - ISNULL(L.DEBIT, 0) END
END) AS ACTUAL,
      (CASE WHEN AE.SIDE = 'Debit' THEN
                  ISNULL(L.DEBIT, 0) - ISNULL(L.CREDIT, 0) ELSE
                  ISNULL(L.CREDIT, 0) - ISNULL(L.DEBIT, 0) END) AS
ACTUAL_YTD,
      0 AS BUDGET,
      0 AS BUDGET_YTD
FROM
      ACCOUNTING_EQUATION AS AE
JOIN
      ACCOUNT AS A
      ON    AE.ELEMENT_ID = A.ELEMENT_ID
JOIN
      LEDGER AS L
      ON    A.ACCT_KEY = L.ACCT_KEY AND
            L.MNTH_ID BETWEEN ROUND(@MNTH_ID, -2) AND
@MNTH_ID
WHERE
      AE.ELEMENT IN ('Revenue', 'Expenses') AND
      L.MNTH_ID BETWEEN ROUND(@MNTH_ID, -2) AND
@MNTH_ID
UNION ALL
SELECT
      AE.ELEMENT, A.ACCT_ID, A.ACCT_NAME,
      0 AS ACTUAL,
      0 AS ACTUAL_YTD,
      (CASE WHEN B.MNTH_ID = @MNTH_ID THEN
            CASE WHEN AE.SIDE = 'Debit' THEN
                  ISNULL(B.DEBIT, 0) - ISNULL(B.CREDIT, 0) ELSE
                  ISNULL(B.CREDIT, 0) - ISNULL(B.DEBIT, 0) END
END) AS BUDGET,
      (CASE WHEN AE.SIDE = 'Debit' THEN
                  ISNULL(B.DEBIT, 0) - ISNULL(B.CREDIT, 0) ELSE
                  ISNULL(B.CREDIT, 0) - ISNULL(B.DEBIT, 0) END) AS
BUDGET_YTD
FROM
      ACCOUNTING_EQUATION AS AE
```

```
JOIN
      ACCOUNT AS A
      ON    AE.ELEMENT_ID = A.ELEMENT_ID
JOIN
      BUDGET AS B
      ON    A.ACCT_KEY = B.ACCT_KEY AND
            B.MNTH_ID BETWEEN ROUND(@MNTH_ID, -2) AND
@MNTH_ID
WHERE
      AE.ELEMENT IN ('Revenue', 'Expenses') AND
      B.MNTH_ID BETWEEN ROUND(@MNTH_ID, -2) AND
@MNTH_ID
)
SELECT
      ELEMENT, ACCT_ID, ACCT_NAME,
      SUM(ACTUAL) AS ACTUAL,
      SUM(BUDGET) AS BUDGET,
      SUM(ACTUAL_YTD) AS ACTUAL_YTD,
      SUM(BUDGET_YTD) AS BUDGET_YTD
FROM
      RSLT
GROUP BY
      ELEMENT, ACCT_ID, ACCT_NAME
ORDER BY
      ACCT_ID
```

The query produces the following resultset:

ELEMENT	ACCT_ID	ACCT_NAME	ACTUAL	BUDGET	ACTUAL_YTD	BUDGET_YTD
Revenue	4000	Consultancy revenue	25800.00	31556.00	40400.00	63112.00
Revenue	4010	Interest earned	51.23	77.00	51.23	154.00
Expenses	5000	Office rent	1600.00	2080.00	3200.00	4160.00
Expenses	5010	Staff salaries	12500.00	16250.00	25000.00	32500.00
Expenses	5020	Utilities	317.95	332.00	418.95	664.00
Expenses	5030	Travel	0.00	85.00	0.00	170.00
Expenses	5035	Office sundries	0.00	84.00	0.00	168.00
Expenses	5040	Loan Interest	77.77	452.00	155.54	904.00
Expenses	5050	Bank Charges	12.50	16.00	12.50	32.00

Cash-flow forecasting

A cash flow forecast estimates cash inflows and outflows for each month. It is similar to a budget, but rather than estimating revenues and expenses, it forecasts the cash that will come in and go out.

The CF_FORECAST table, described below, holds monthly estimates of cash movements:

Column Name	Description	Type	Length	Null	Key	Foreign Table
ROW_NUM	Unique Id	bigint		N	P	
MNTH_ID	Month Id	int		N	F	FISCAL_MONTH
CF_ID	Cash flow category ID	int		N	F	CF_CATEGORY
DEBIT	Cash inflow (If any)	money		Y		
CREDIT	Cash outflow (if any)	money		Y		

Cash estimates for the first two months of the fiscal year 2024 can be recorded in the table CF_FORECAST as follows:

ROW_NUM	MNTH_ID	CF_ID	DEBIT	CREDIT
1	202401	1	10735.00	
2	202401	2	49.00	
3	202401	3		8800.00
4	202401	4		4950.00
5	202401	5		511.00
6	202401	6		12000.00
7	202401	8	18000.00	
8	202401	9	35000.00	
9	202401	10		650.00
10	202401	11		
11	202402	1	10735.00	
12	202402	2	49.00	
13	202402	3		8800.00
14	202402	4		4950.00
15	202402	5		511.00
16	202402	6		2000.00
17	202402	8		
18	202402	9		
19	202402	10		650.00
20	202402	11		

The debit column stores estimates of inflows, whilst the credit column holds the outflows of cash.

Below is an example of a cash flow variance analysis report for the second month of the fiscal year 2024:

Murewa Consultancy Cash Flow Variance Analysis for month ending May 31, 2023			
	Actuals	**Forecast**	**Variance**
Operating Activities			
Cash received from customers	14,350.00	10,735.00	3,615.00
Interest Received	51.23	49.00	2.23
Cash paid to Employees	-8,000.00	-8,800.00	800.00
Cash paid for Income Tax	-4,500.00	-4,950.00	450.00
Cash paid for other operating expenses	-1,612.50	-511.00	-1,101.50
Net cash from Operating Activities [A]	**288.73**	**-3,477.00**	**3,765.73**
Investing Activities			
Purchase of Property and Equipment	0.00	-2,000.00	2,000.00
Sale of property and equipment	0.00	0.00	0.00
Net cash from Investing Activities [B]	**0.00**	**-2,000.00**	**2,000.00**
Financing Activities			
Add: Investment by the owner	0.00	0.00	0.00
Add: long-term debt	0.00	0.00	0.00
Less: Repayments of long-term debt	-577.77	-650.00	72.23
Less: Withdrawals by the owner	0.00	0.00	0.00
Net cash from Financing Activities [C]	**-577.77**	**-650.00**	**72.23**
Increase / Decrease in cash and cash equivalents (A+B+C)	**-289.04**	**-6,127.00**	**5,837.96**

The following is an example of the T-SQL data retrieval code:

```
DECLARE     @MNTH_ID        INT = 202402
;
WITH RSLT AS
(
SELECT
        A.ACTIVITY_ID, A.ACTIVITY + ' Activities' AS ACTIVITY,
        H.CF_ID,
        H.CATEGORY,
        SUM(ISNULL(S.DEBIT, 0) - ISNULL(S.CREDIT, 0)) AS AMOUNT,
        0 AS FORECAST
FROM
        ACTIVITY AS A
JOIN
        CF_CATEGORY AS H
        ON     A.ACTIVITY_ID = H.ACTIVITY_ID
LEFT JOIN
        JOURNAL AS S
        ON     H.CF_ID = S.CF_ID AND
               S.MNTH_ID = @MNTH_ID
GROUP BY
        A.ACTIVITY_ID, A.ACTIVITY + ' Activities',
        H.CF_ID,
```

```
        H.CATEGORY
UNION
SELECT
        A.ACTIVITY_ID, A.ACTIVITY + ' Activities' AS ACTIVITY,
        H.CF_ID,
        H.CATEGORY,
        0 AS AMOUNT,
        SUM(ISNULL(S.DEBIT, 0) - ISNULL(S.CREDIT, 0)) AS FORECAST
FROM
        ACTIVITY AS A
JOIN
        CF_CATEGORY AS H
        ON      A.ACTIVITY_ID = H.ACTIVITY_ID
LEFT JOIN
        CF_FORECAST AS S
        ON      H.CF_ID = S.CF_ID AND
                S.MNTH_ID = @MNTH_ID
GROUP BY
        A.ACTIVITY_ID, A.ACTIVITY + ' Activities',
        H.CF_ID,
        H.CATEGORY
)
SELECT
        ACTIVITY_ID, ACTIVITY,
        CF_ID,
        CATEGORY,
        SUM(AMOUNT) AS AMOUNT,
        SUM(FORECAST) AS FORECAST
FROM
        RSLT
GROUP BY
        ACTIVITY_ID, ACTIVITY,
        CF_ID,
        CATEGORY
ORDER BY
        1, 3
```

The resultset is as follows:

ACTIVITY_ID	ACTIVITY	CF_ID	CATEGORY	AMOUNT	FORECAST
1	Operating Activities	1	Cash received from customers	14350.00	10735.00
1	Operating Activities	2	Interest received	51.23	49.00
1	Operating Activities	3	Cash paid to Employees	-8000.00	-8800.00
1	Operating Activities	4	Cash paid for Income Tax	-4500.00	-4950.00
1	Operating Activities	5	Cash paid for other operating expenses	-1612.50	-511.00
2	Investing Activities	6	Purchase of property and equipment	0.00	-2000.00
2	Investing Activities	7	Sale of property and equipment	0.00	0.00
3	Financing Activities	8	Add: Investment by the owner	0.00	0.00
3	Financing Activities	9	Add: long-term debt	0.00	0.00
3	Financing Activities	10	Less: Repayments of long-term debt	-577.77	-650.00
3	Financing Activities	11	Less: Withdrawals by the owner	0.00	0.00

Appendix

May 2023 answers

1. Office rent payment. Accounts Payable and Expenses module.

   ```
   exec sp_Process_Trans
       @TRAN_TYPE_ID    = 12,
       @TRAN_DATE = '3 May 2023',
       @REF_ID        = 'PR-2',
       @AMOUNT      = 1600.00
   ```

2. Interest earned. Banking module.

   ```
   exec sp_Process_Trans
       @TRAN_TYPE_ID    = 23,
       @TRAN_DATE = '6 May 2023',
       @REF_ID        = '1023',
       @AMOUNT      = 51.23
   ```

3. Customer invoice. Accounts Receivable module.

   ```
   exec sp_Process_Trans
       @TRAN_TYPE_ID    = 15,
       @TRAN_DATE = '9 May 2023',
       @REF_ID        = '772',
       @AMOUNT      = 14600.00
   ```

4. Client cash receipt. Accounts Receivable module.

   ```
   exec sp_Process_Trans
       @TRAN_TYPE_ID    = 16,
       @TRAN_DATE  = '10 May 2023',
       @REF_ID        = '512',
       @AMOUNT      = 9850.00
   ```

5. Customer invoice. Accounts Receivable module.

   ```
   exec sp_Process_Trans
       @TRAN_TYPE_ID    = 15,
       @TRAN_DATE = '11 May 2023',
       @REF_ID        = '773',
       @AMOUNT      = 11200.00
   ```

6. Utility bill. Accounts Payable and Expenses module.

   ```
   exec sp_Process_Trans
       @TRAN_TYPE_ID    = 10,
       @TRAN_DATE  = '13 May 2023',
       @REF_ID        = '254',
       @AMOUNT      = 101.00
   ```

7. Client cash receipt. Accounts Receivable module.

   ```
   exec sp_Process_Trans
       @TRAN_TYPE_ID    = 16,
       @TRAN_DATE  = '19 May 2023',
       @REF_ID        = '881',
       @AMOUNT      = 4500.00
   ```

8. Monthly payroll. Payroll Module.

   ```
   exec sp_Process_Trans
       @TRAN_TYPE_ID    = 17,
       @TRAN_DATE  = '24 May 2023',
       @REF_ID        = '05/24',
       @AMOUNT      = 12500.00,
       @INCOME_TAX = 4500.00,
       @NET_PAY     = 8000.00
   ```

9. Income tax payment. Payroll module.
    exec sp_Process_Trans
        @TRAN_TYPE_ID   = 18,
        @TRAN_DATE = '25 May 2023',
        @REF_ID   = '05/24',
        @AMOUNT   = 4500.00

10. Net salary payment. Payroll module.
    exec sp_Process_Trans
        @TRAN_TYPE_ID   = 19,
        @TRAN_DATE = '25 May 2023',
        @REF_ID   = '05/24',
        @AMOUNT   = 8000.00

11. Utility bill. Accounts Payable and Expenses module.
    exec sp_Process_Trans
        @TRAN_TYPE_ID   = 10,
        @TRAN_DATE = '29 May 2023',
        @REF_ID   = '1090',
        @AMOUNT   = 93.50

12. Utility bill. Accounts Payable and Expenses module.
    exec sp_Process_Trans
        @TRAN_TYPE_ID   = 10,
        @TRAN_DATE = '30 May 2023',
        @REF_ID   = '611',
        @AMOUNT   = 123.45

13. Long-term loan payment. Business Financing module.
    exec sp_Process_Trans
        @TRAN_TYPE_ID   = 4,
        @TRAN_DATE = '31 May 2023',
        @REF_ID   = 'LTP-2',
        @AMOUNT   = 577.77,
        @INTEREST   = 77.77,
        @PRINCIPAL = 500.00

14. Bank charges payment. Banking module.

    exec sp_Process_Trans
        @TRAN_TYPE_ID   = 22,
        @TRAN_DATE = '31 May 2023',
        @REF_ID   = ' BC1',
        @AMOUNT   = 12.50

June 2023 answers

1. Office rent payment. Accounts Payable and Expenses module.
    exec sp_Process_Trans
        @TRAN_TYPE_ID   = 12,
        @TRAN_DATE= '2 Jun 2023',
        @REF_ID   = 'PR-3',
        @AMOUNT   = 1600.00

2. Interest earned. Banking module.

    exec sp_Process_Trans
        @TRAN_TYPE_ID   = 23,
        @TRAN_DATE= '6 Jun 2023',
        @REF_ID   = '1024',
        @AMOUNT   = 51.23

3. Utility bill payment. Accounts Payable and Expenses module.

   ```
   exec sp_Process_Trans
       @TRAN_TYPE_ID    = 11,
       @TRAN_DATE = '8 Jun 2023',
       @REF_ID        = '1091',
       @AMOUNT     = 93.50
   ```

4. Utility bill payment. Accounts Payable and Expenses module.

   ```
   exec sp_Process_Trans
       @TRAN_TYPE_ID    = 11,
       @TRAN_DATE = '9 Jun 2023',
       @REF_ID        = '611P ',
       @AMOUNT     = 133.45
   ```

5. Customer invoice. Accounts Receivable module.

   ```
   exec sp_Process_Trans
       @TRAN_TYPE_ID    = 15,
       @TRAN_DATE = '10 Jun 2023',
       @REF_ID        = '773',
       @AMOUNT     = 14700.00
   ```

6. Client cash receipt. Accounts Receivable module.

   ```
   exec sp_Process_Trans
       @TRAN_TYPE_ID    = 16,
       @TRAN_DATE = '11 Jun 2023',
       @REF_ID        = '514',
       @AMOUNT     = 10500.00
   ```

7. Client cash receipt. Accounts Receivable module.

   ```
   exec sp_Process_Trans
       @TRAN_TYPE_ID    = 16,
       @TRAN_DATE = '19 Jun 2023',
       @REF_ID        = '882',
       @AMOUNT     = 8450.00
   ```

8. Monthly payroll. Payroll Module.

   ```
   exec sp_Process_Trans
       @TRAN_TYPE_ID    = 17,
       @TRAN_DATE = '23 Jun 2023',
       @REF_ID        = '06/24',
       @AMOUNT     = 12500.00,
       @INCOME_TAX = 4500.00,
       @NET_PAY     = 8000.00
   ```

9. Income tax payment. Payroll module.

   ```
   exec sp_Process_Trans
       @TRAN_TYPE_ID    = 18,
       @TRAN_DATE = '24 Jun 2023',
       @REF_ID        = '06/24',
       @AMOUNT     = 4500.00
   ```

10. Net salary payment. Payroll module.

    ```
    exec sp_Process_Trans
        @TRAN_TYPE_ID    = 19,
        @TRAN_DATE = '24 Jun 2023',
        @REF_ID        = '06/24',
        @AMOUNT     = 8000.00
    ```

11. Utility bill. Accounts Payable and Expenses module.

    ```
    exec sp_Process_Trans
        @TRAN_TYPE_ID    = 10,
        @TRAN_DATE = '28 Jun 2023',
        @REF_ID        = '1091',
        @AMOUNT     = 98.50
    ```

12. Utility bill. Accounts Payable and Expenses module.

    ```
    exec sp_Process_Trans
        @TRAN_TYPE_ID    = 10,
        @TRAN_DATE = '30 Jun 2023',
        @REF_ID        = '612',
        @AMOUNT     = 144.50
    ```

13. Long-term loan payment. Business Financing module.

```
exec sp_Process_Trans
    @TRAN_TYPE_ID    = 4,
    @TRAN_DATE = '30 Jun 2023',
    @REF_ID      = 'LTP-3',
    @AMOUNT      = 577.77,
    @INTEREST    = 77.77,
    @PRINCIPAL   = 500.00
```

14. Bank charges payment. Banking module.

```
exec sp_Process_Trans
    @TRAN_TYPE_ID    = 22,
    @TRAN_DATE = '30 Jun 2023',
    @REF_ID      = ' BC-2',
    @AMOUNT      = 12.50
```

July 2023 answers

1. Office rent payment. Accounts Payable and Expenses module.

```
exec sp_Process_Trans
    @TRAN_TYPE_ID    = 12,
    @TRAN_DATE= '2 Jul 2023',
    @REF_ID      = 'PR-4',
    @AMOUNT      = 1600.00
```

2. Interest earned. Banking module.

```
exec sp_Process_Trans
    @TRAN_TYPE_ID    = 23,
    @TRAN_DATE= '6 Jul 2023',
    @REF_ID      = '1025',
    @AMOUNT      = 51.22
```

3. Utility bill payment. Accounts Payable and Expenses module.

```
exec sp_Process_Trans
    @TRAN_TYPE_ID    = 11,
    @TRAN_DATE= '8 Jul 2023',
    @REF_ID      = '1092',
    @AMOUNT      = 98.50
```

4. Utility bill payment. Accounts Payable and Expenses module.

```
exec sp_Process_Trans
    @TRAN_TYPE_ID    = 11,
    @TRAN_DATE= '9 Jul 2023',
    @REF_ID      = '611P ',
    @AMOUNT      = 144.50
```

5. Owner cash withdrawal. Business finance module.

```
exec sp_Process_Trans
    @TRAN_TYPE_ID    = 2,
    @TRAN_DATE= '10 Jul 2023',
    @REF_ID      = 'CW-1',
    @AMOUNT      = 1500.00
```

6. Customer invoice. Accounts Receivable module.

```
exec sp_Process_Trans
    @TRAN_TYPE_ID    = 15,
    @TRAN_DATE= '12 Jul 2023',
    @REF_ID      = '774',
    @AMOUNT      = 16700.00
```

7. Client cash receipt. Accounts Receivable module.

```
exec sp_Process_Trans
    @TRAN_TYPE_ID    = 16,
    @TRAN_DATE = '13 Jul 2023',
    @REF_ID      = '515',
    @AMOUNT      = 10500.00
```

8. Monthly payroll. Payroll Module.

```
exec sp_Process_Trans
    @TRAN_TYPE_ID    = 17,
    @TRAN_DATE = '23 Jul 2023',
    @REF_ID      = '07/24',
    @AMOUNT      = 12500.00,
    @INCOME_TAX = 4500.00,
    @NET_PAY     = 8000.00
```

9. Income tax payment. Payroll module.
```
exec sp_Process_Trans
     @TRAN_TYPE_ID    = 18,
     @TRAN_DATE = '24 Jul 2023',
     @REF_ID        = '07/24',
     @AMOUNT       = 4500.00
```

10. Net salary payment. Payroll module.
```
exec sp_Process_Trans
     @TRAN_TYPE_ID    = 19,
     @TRAN_DATE = '24 Jul 2023',
     @REF_ID        = '07/24',
     @AMOUNT       = 8000.00
```

11. Utility bill. Accounts Payable and Expenses module.
```
exec sp_Process_Trans
     @TRAN_TYPE_ID    = 10,
     @TRAN_DATE = '28 Jul 2023',
     @REF_ID        = '1092',
     @AMOUNT       = 98.50
```

12. Utility bill. Accounts Payable and Expenses module.
```
exec sp_Process_Trans
     @TRAN_TYPE_ID    = 10,
     @TRAN_DATE = '30 Jul 2023',
     @REF_ID        = '613',
     @AMOUNT       = 144.50
```

13. Long-term loan payment. Business Financing module.
```
exec sp_Process_Trans
     @TRAN_TYPE_ID    = 4,
     @TRAN_DATE = '31 Jul 2023',
     @REF_ID        = 'LTP-4',
     @AMOUNT       = 577.77,
     @INTEREST     = 77.77,
     @PRINCIPAL   = 500.00
```

14. Bank charges payment. Banking module.
```
exec sp_Process_Trans
     @TRAN_TYPE_ID    = 22,
     @TRAN_DATE = '31 Jul 2023',
     @REF_ID        = ' BC-3',
     @AMOUNT       = 12.50
```

August 2023 answers

1. Office rent payment. Accounts Payable and Expenses module.
```
exec sp_Process_Trans
     @TRAN_TYPE_ID    = 12,
     @TRAN_DATE= '2 Aug 2023',
     @REF_ID        = 'PR-5',
     @AMOUNT       = 1600.00
```

2. Interest earned. Banking module.
```
exec sp_Process_Trans
     @TRAN_TYPE_ID    = 23,
     @TRAN_DATE= '6 Aug 2023',
     @REF_ID        = '1026',
     @AMOUNT       = 51.22
```

3. Utility bill payment. Accounts Payable and Expenses module.
```
exec sp_Process_Trans
     @TRAN_TYPE_ID    = 11,
     @TRAN_DATE= '8 Aug 2023',
     @REF_ID        = '1093',
     @AMOUNT       = 102.00
```

4. Utility bill payment. Accounts Payable and Expenses module.
```
exec sp_Process_Trans
     @TRAN_TYPE_ID    = 11,
     @TRAN_DATE= '9 Aug 2023',
     @REF_ID        = '612P ',
     @AMOUNT       = 164.99
```

5. Customer invoice. Accounts Receivable module.

```
exec sp_Process_Trans
    @TRAN_TYPE_ID    = 15,
    @TRAN_DATE = '12 Aug 2023',
    @REF_ID       = '775',
    @AMOUNT    = 17300.00
```

6. Customer invoice. Accounts Receivable module.

```
exec sp_Process_Trans
    @TRAN_TYPE_ID    = 15,
    @TRAN_DATE = '13 Aug 2023',
    @REF_ID       = '776',
    @AMOUNT    = 18200.00
```

7. Client cash receipt. Accounts Receivable module.

```
exec sp_Process_Trans
    @TRAN_TYPE_ID = 16,
    @TRAN_DATE = '15 Aug 2023',
    @REF_ID       = '516',
    @AMOUNT    = 11200.00
```

8. Customer invoice. Accounts Receivable module.

```
exec sp_Process_Trans
    @TRAN_TYPE_ID    = 15,
    @TRAN_DATE = '15 Aug 2023',
    @REF_ID       = '776-Y',
    @AMOUNT    = 18200.00
```

9. Mortgage loan. Business finance module.

```
exec sp_Process_Trans
    @TRAN_TYPE_ID    = 5,
    @TRAN_DATE = '16 Aug 2023',
    @REF_ID       = 'ML-1',
    @AMOUNT    = 80000.00
```

10. Monthly payroll. Payroll module.

```
exec sp_Process_Trans
    @TRAN_TYPE_ID    = 17,
    @TRAN_DATE = '23 Aug 2023',
    @REF_ID       = '08/24',
    @AMOUNT    = 12500.00,
    @INCOME_TAX = 4500.00,
    @NET_PAY     = 8000.00
```

11. Net salary payment. Payroll module.

```
exec sp_Process_Trans
    @TRAN_TYPE_ID    = 19,
    @TRAN_DATE = '24 Aug 2023',
    @REF_ID       = '08/24',
    @AMOUNT    = 8000.00
```

12. Income tax payment. Payroll module.

```
exec sp_Process_Trans
    @TRAN_TYPE_ID    = 18,
    @TRAN_DATE = '24 Aug 2023',
    @REF_ID       = '08/24',
    @AMOUNT    = 4500.00
```

13. Utility bill. Accounts Payable and Expenses module.

```
exec sp_Process_Trans
    @TRAN_TYPE_ID    = 10,
    @TRAN_DATE = '28 Aug 2023',
    @REF_ID       = '1093',
    @AMOUNT    = 103.00
```

14. Utility bill. Accounts Payable and Expenses module.

```
exec sp_Process_Trans
    @TRAN_TYPE_ID    = 10,
    @TRAN_DATE = '30 Aug 2023',
    @REF_ID       = '614',
    @AMOUNT    = 166.50
```

15. Long-term loan payment. Business Financing module.

```
exec sp_Process_Trans
    @TRAN_TYPE_ID   = 4,
    @TRAN_DATE = '31 Aug 2023',
    @REF_ID       = 'LTP-5',
    @AMOUNT     = 577.77,
    @INTEREST    = 77.77,
    @PRINCIPAL   = 500.00
```

16. Bank charges payment. Banking module.

```
exec sp_Process_Trans
    @TRAN_TYPE_ID   = 22,
    @TRAN_DATE = '31 Aug 2023',
    @REF_ID       = ' BC-4',
    @AMOUNT     = 12.50
```

September 2023 answers

1. Office rent payment. Accounts Payable and Expenses module.

```
exec sp_Process_Trans
    @TRAN_TYPE_ID   = 12,
    @TRAN_DATE = '2 Sep 2023',
    @REF_ID       = 'PR-6',
    @AMOUNT     = 1600.00
```

2. Interest earned. Banking module.

```
exec sp_Process_Trans
    @TRAN_TYPE_ID   = 23,
    @TRAN_DATE = '6 Sep 2023',
    @REF_ID       = '1027',
    @AMOUNT     = 51.22
```

3. Utility bill payment. Accounts Payable and Expenses module.

```
exec sp_Process_Trans
    @TRAN_TYPE_ID   = 11,
    @TRAN_DATE = '8 Sep 2023',
    @REF_ID       = '1093',
    @AMOUNT     = 103.00
```

4. Utility bill payment. Accounts Payable and Expenses module.

```
exec sp_Process_Trans
    @TRAN_TYPE_ID   = 11,
    @TRAN_DATE = '9 Sep 2023',
    @REF_ID       = '613P',
    @AMOUNT     = 166.50
```

5. Customer invoice. Accounts Receivable module.

```
exec sp_Process_Trans
    @TRAN_TYPE_ID   = 15,
    @TRAN_DATE = '11 Sep 2023',
    @REF_ID       = '518 ',
    @AMOUNT     = 10500.00
```

6. Vehicles purchase. Asset management module.

```
exec sp_Process_Trans
    @TRAN_TYPE_ID   = 9,
    @TRAN_DATE = '12 Sep 2023',
    @REF_ID       = 'VP-1',
    @AMOUNT     = 6500.00
```

7. Customer invoice. Accounts Receivable module.

```
exec sp_Process_Trans
    @TRAN_TYPE_ID   = 15,
    @TRAN_DATE = '13 Sep 2023',
    @REF_ID       = '777',
    @AMOUNT     = 18200.00
```

8. Mortgage loan payment. Business Finance module.

```
exec sp_Process_Trans
    @TRAN_TYPE_ID   = 6,
    @TRAN_DATE = '16 Sep 2023',
    @REF_ID       = 'MP-1',
    @AMOUNT     = 1565.00,
    @INTEREST    = 462.00,
    @PRINCIPAL   = 1103.00
```

9. Monthly payroll. Payroll Module.
```
exec sp_Process_Trans
    @TRAN_TYPE_ID      = 17,
    @TRAN_DATE = '23 Sep 2023',
    @REF_ID        = '09/24',
    @AMOUNT       = 12500.00,
    @INCOME_TAX = 4500.00,
    @NET_PAY      = 8000.00
```

10. Net salary payment. Payroll module.
```
exec sp_Process_Trans
    @TRAN_TYPE_ID       = 19,
    @TRAN_DATE = '24 Sep 2023',
    @REF_ID        = '09/24',
    @AMOUNT       = 8000.00
```

11. Income tax payment. Payroll module.
```
exec sp_Process_Trans
    @TRAN_TYPE_ID      = 18,
    @TRAN_DATE = '24 Sep 2023',
    @REF_ID        = '09/24',
    @AMOUNT       = 4500.00
```

12. Utility bill. Accounts Payable and Expenses module.
```
exec sp_Process_Trans
    @TRAN_TYPE_ID       = 10,
    @TRAN_DATE = '28 Sep 2023',
    @REF_ID        = '1094',
    @AMOUNT       = 103.00
```

13. Utility bill. Accounts Payable and Expenses module.
```
exec sp_Process_Trans
    @TRAN_TYPE_ID      = 10,
    @TRAN_DATE = '30 Sep 2023',
    @REF_ID        = '615',
    @AMOUNT       = 166.50
```

14. Long-term loan payment. Business Financing module.
```
exec sp_Process_Trans
    @TRAN_TYPE_ID       = 4,
    @TRAN_DATE = '30 Sep 2023',
    @REF_ID        = 'LTP-6',
    @AMOUNT       = 577.77,
    @INTEREST     = 77.77,
    @PRINCIPAL    = 500.00
```

15. Bank charges payment. Banking module.
```
exec sp_Process_Trans
    @TRAN_TYPE_ID       = 22,
    @TRAN_DATE = '30 Sep 2023',
    @REF_ID        = ' BC-5',
    @AMOUNT       = 12.50
```

16. Client cash receipt. Accounts receivable module.
```
exec sp_Process_Trans
    @TRAN_TYPE_ID       = 16,
    @TRAN_DATE = '30 Sep 2023',
    @REF_ID        = '518-2',
    @AMOUNT       = 16000.00
```

October 2023 answers

1. Office rent payment. Accounts Payable and Expenses module.
   ```
   exec sp_Process_Trans
       @TRAN_TYPE_ID   = 12,
       @TRAN_DATE = '2 Oct 2023',
       @REF_ID         = 'PR-7',
       @AMOUNT     = 1600.00
   ```

2. Interest earned. Banking module.
   ```
   exec sp_Process_Trans
       @TRAN_TYPE_ID   = 23,
       @TRAN_DATE = '6 Oct 2023',
       @REF_ID         = '1028',
       @AMOUNT     = 51.22
   ```

3. Utility bill payment. Accounts Payable and Expenses module.
   ```
   exec sp_Process_Trans
       @TRAN_TYPE_ID   = 11,
       @TRAN_DATE = '8 Oct 2023',
       @REF_ID         = '1094',
       @AMOUNT     = 103.00
   ```

4. Utility bill payment. Accounts Payable and Expenses module.
   ```
   exec sp_Process_Trans
       @TRAN_TYPE_ID   = 11,
       @TRAN_DATE = '9 Oct 2023',
       @REF_ID         = '614P',
       @AMOUNT     = 166.50
   ```

5. Client cash receipt. Accounts Receivable module.
   ```
   exec sp_Process_Trans
       @TRAN_TYPE_ID   = 16,
       @TRAN_DATE = '11 Oct 2023',
       @REF_ID         = '519',
       @AMOUNT     = 8000.00
   ```

6. Customer invoice. Accounts Receivable module.
   ```
   exec sp_Process_Trans
       @TRAN_TYPE_ID   = 15,
       @TRAN_DATE = '14 Oct 2023',
       @REF_ID         = '778',
       @AMOUNT     = 18200.00
   ```

7. Mortgage loan payment. Business Finance module.
   ```
   exec sp_Process_Trans
       @TRAN_TYPE_ID    = 6,
       @TRAN_DATE =  '16 Oct 2023',
       @REF_ID         = 'MP-2',
       @AMOUNT     = 1565.00,
       @INTEREST   = 462.50,
       @PRINCIPAL  = 1102.50
   ```

8. Monthly payroll. Payroll Module.
   ```
   exec sp_Process_Trans
       @TRAN_TYPE_ID     = 17,
       @TRAN_DATE =  '23 Oct 2023',
       @REF_ID         = '10/24',
       @AMOUNT     = 12500.00,
       @INCOME_TAX = 4500.00,
       @NET_PAY        = 8000.00
   ```

9. Net salary payment. Payroll module.
   ```
   exec sp_Process_Trans
       @TRAN_TYPE_ID     = 19,
       @TRAN_DATE =  '24 Oct 2023',
       @REF_ID         = '10/24',
       @AMOUNT     = 8000.00
   ```

10. Income tax payment. Payroll module.
    ```
    exec sp_Process_Trans
        @TRAN_TYPE_ID     = 18,
        @TRAN_DATE =  '24 Oct 2023',
        @REF_ID         = '10/24',
        @AMOUNT     = 4500.00
    ```

11. Utility bill. Accounts Payable and Expenses module.

```
exec sp_Process_Trans
    @TRAN_TYPE_ID    = 10,
    @TRAN_DATE = '28 Oct 2023',
    @REF_ID        = '1095',
    @AMOUNT        = 103.00
```

12. Utility bill. Accounts Payable and Expenses module.

```
exec sp_Process_Trans
    @TRAN_TYPE_ID    = 10,
    @TRAN_DATE = '31 Oct 2023',
    @REF_ID        = '616',
    @AMOUNT        = 166.50
```

13. Long-term loan payment. Business Financing module.

```
exec sp_Process_Trans
    @TRAN_TYPE_ID    = 4,
    @TRAN_DATE = '31 Oct 2023',
    @REF_ID        = 'LTP-7',
    @AMOUNT        = 577.77,
    @INTEREST      = 77.77,
    @PRINCIPAL     = 500.00
```

14. Bank charges payment. Banking module.

```
exec sp_Process_Trans
    @TRAN_TYPE_ID    = 22,
    @TRAN_DATE = '31 Oct 2023',
    @REF_ID        = ' BC-6',
    @AMOUNT        = 12.50
```

15. Client cash receipt. Accounts Receivable module.

```
exec sp_Process_Trans
    @TRAN_TYPE_ID    = 16,
    @TRAN_DATE= '31 Oct 2023',
    @REF_ID        = '519-2',
    @AMOUNT        = 18500.00
```

November 2023 answers

1. Office rent payment. Accounts Payable and Expenses module.

```
exec sp_Process_Trans
    @TRAN_TYPE_ID    = 12,
    @TRAN_DATE= '2 Nov 2023',
    @REF_ID        = 'PR-8',
    @AMOUNT        = 1600.00
```

2. Interest earned. Banking module.

```
exec sp_Process_Trans
    @TRAN_TYPE_ID    = 23,
    @TRAN_DATE= '6 Nov 2023',
    @REF_ID        = '1029',
    @AMOUNT        = 51.22
```

3. Utility bill payment. Accounts Payable and Expenses module.

```
exec sp_Process_Trans
    @TRAN_TYPE_ID    = 11,
    @TRAN_DATE= '8 Nov 2023',
    @REF_ID        = '1095',
    @AMOUNT        = 103.00
```

4. Utility bill payment. Accounts Payable and Expenses module.

```
exec sp_Process_Trans
    @TRAN_TYPE_ID    = 11,
    @TRAN_DATE= '9 Nov 2023',
    @REF_ID        = '615P',
    @AMOUNT        = 166.50
```

5. Travel / Fuel payment. Accounts Payable and Expenses module.

```
exec sp_Process_Trans
    @TRAN_TYPE_ID    = 13,
    @TRAN_DATE = '11 Nov 2023',
    @REF_ID        = '3356',
    @AMOUNT    = 65.00
```

6. Client cash receipt. Accounts Receivable module.

```
exec sp_Process_Trans
    @TRAN_TYPE_ID    = 16,
    @TRAN_DATE = '12 Nov 2023',
    @REF_ID        = '520',
    @AMOUNT    = 16200.00
```

7. Customer invoice. Accounts Receivable module.

```
exec sp_Process_Trans
    @TRAN_TYPE_ID    = 15,
    @TRAN_DATE = '15 Nov 2023',
    @REF_ID        = '779',
    @AMOUNT    = 15500.00
```

8. Mortgage loan payment. Business Finance module.

```
exec sp_Process_Trans
    @TRAN_TYPE_ID    = 6,
    @TRAN_DATE = '16 Nov 2023',
    @REF_ID        = 'MP-3',
    @AMOUNT    = 1565.00,
    @INTEREST    = 462.75,
    @PRINCIPAL    = 1102.25
```

9. Monthly payroll. Payroll Module.

```
exec sp_Process_Trans
    @TRAN_TYPE_ID    = 17,
    @TRAN_DATE = '23 Nov 2023',
    @REF_ID        = '11/24',
    @AMOUNT    = 12500.00,
    @INCOME_TAX = 4500.00,
    @NET_PAY    = 8000.00
```

10. Net salary payment. Payroll module.

```
exec sp_Process_Trans
    @TRAN_TYPE_ID    = 19,
    @TRAN_DATE = '24 Nov 2023',
    @REF_ID        = '11/24',
    @AMOUNT    = 8000.00
```

11. Income tax payment. Payroll module.

```
exec sp_Process_Trans
    @TRAN_TYPE_ID    = 18,
    @TRAN_DATE = '24 Nov 2023',
    @REF_ID        = '11/24',
    @AMOUNT    = 4500.00
```

12. Utility bill. Accounts Payable and Expenses module.

```
exec sp_Process_Trans
    @TRAN_TYPE_ID    = 10,
    @TRAN_DATE = '28 Nov 2023',
    @REF_ID        = '1096',
    @AMOUNT    = 103.00
```

13. Utility bill. Accounts Payable and Expenses module.

```
exec sp_Process_Trans
    @TRAN_TYPE_ID    = 10,
    @TRAN_DATE = '30 Nov 2023',
    @REF_ID        = '617',
    @AMOUNT    = 166.50
```

14. Long-term loan payment. Business Financing module.

```
exec sp_Process_Trans
    @TRAN_TYPE_ID    = 4,
    @TRAN_DATE = '30 Nov 2023',
    @REF_ID        = 'LTP-8',
    @AMOUNT    = 577.77,
    @INTEREST    = 77.77,
    @PRINCIPAL    = 500.00
```

15. Bank charges payment. Banking module.

```
exec sp_Process_Trans
    @TRAN_TYPE_ID    = 22,
    @TRAN_DATE = '30 Nov 2023',
    @REF_ID       = ' BC-7',
    @AMOUNT       = 12.50
```

December 2023 answers

1. Office rent payment. Accounts Payable and Expenses module.

```
exec sp_Process_Trans
    @TRAN_TYPE_ID    = 12,
    @TRAN_DATE= '2 Dec 2023',
    @REF_ID       = 'PR-9',
    @AMOUNT       = 1600.00
```

2. Interest earned. Banking module.

```
exec sp_Process_Trans
    @TRAN_TYPE_ID    = 23,
    @TRAN_DATE= '6 Dec 2023',
    @REF_ID       = '1030',
    @AMOUNT       = 51.22
```

3. Utility bill payment. Accounts Payable and Expenses module.

```
exec sp_Process_Trans
    @TRAN_TYPE_ID    = 11,
    @TRAN_DATE= '8 Dec 2023',
    @REF_ID       = '1096',
    @AMOUNT       = 103.00
```

4. Utility bill payment. Accounts Payable and Expenses module.

```
exec sp_Process_Trans
    @TRAN_TYPE_ID    = 11,
    @TRAN_DATE= '9 Dec 2023',
    @REF_ID       = '616P',
    @AMOUNT       = 166.50
```

5. Customer invoice. Accounts Receivable module.

```
exec sp_Process_Trans
    @TRAN_TYPE_ID    = 15,
    @TRAN_DATE= '11 Dec 2023',
    @REF_ID       = '780 ',
    @AMOUNT       = 12500.00
```

6. Mortgage loan payment. Business Finance module.

```
exec sp_Process_Trans
    @TRAN_TYPE_ID    = 6,
    @TRAN_DATE = '16 Dec 2023',
    @REF_ID       = 'MP-4',
    @AMOUNT       = 1565.00,
    @INTEREST    = 462.75,
    @PRINCIPAL  = 1102.25
```

7. Travel / Fuel payment. Accounts Payable and Expenses module.

```
exec sp_Process_Trans
    @TRAN_TYPE_ID    = 13,
    @TRAN_DATE= '22 Dec 2023',
    @REF_ID       = '3355 ',
    @AMOUNT       = 53.00
```

8. Monthly payroll. Payroll Module.

```
exec sp_Process_Trans
    @TRAN_TYPE_ID    = 17,
    @TRAN_DATE = '23 Dec 2023',
    @REF_ID       = '12/24',
    @AMOUNT       = 12500.00,
    @INCOME_TAX = 4500.00,
    @NET_PAY    = 8000.00
```

9. Net salary payment. Payroll module.
```
exec sp_Process_Trans
    @TRAN_TYPE_ID    = 19,
    @TRAN_DATE = '24 Dec 2023',
    @REF_ID       = '12/24',
    @AMOUNT     = 8000.00
```

10. Income tax payment. Payroll module.
```
exec sp_Process_Trans
    @TRAN_TYPE_ID    = 18,
    @TRAN_DATE = '24 Dec 2023',
    @REF_ID       = '12/24',
    @AMOUNT     = 4500.00
```

11. Client cash receipt. Accounts Receivable module.
```
exec sp_Process_Trans
    @TRAN_TYPE_ID    = 16,
    @TRAN_DATE = '27 Dec 2023',
    @REF_ID       = '522 ',
    @AMOUNT     = 12500.00
```

12. Utility bill. Accounts Payable and Expenses module.
```
exec sp_Process_Trans
    @TRAN_TYPE_ID    = 10,
    @TRAN_DATE = '28 Dec 2023',
    @REF_ID       = '1097',
    @AMOUNT     = 103.00
```

13. Utility bill. Accounts Payable and Expenses module.
```
exec sp_Process_Trans
    @TRAN_TYPE_ID    = 10,
    @TRAN_DATE = '30 Dec 2023',
    @REF_ID       = '618',
    @AMOUNT     = 166.50
```

14. Long-term loan payment. Business Financing module.
```
exec sp_Process_Trans
    @TRAN_TYPE_ID    = 4,
    @TRAN_DATE = '31 Dec 2023',
    @REF_ID       = 'LTP-9',
    @AMOUNT     = 577.77,
    @INTEREST   = 77.77,
    @PRINCIPAL  = 500.00
```

15. Bank charges payment. Banking module.
```
exec sp_Process_Trans
    @TRAN_TYPE_ID    = 22,
    @TRAN_DATE = '31 Dec 2023',
    @REF_ID       = ' BC-8',
    @AMOUNT     = 12.50
```

January 2024 answers

1. Office rent payment. Accounts Payable and Expenses module.
```
exec sp_Process_Trans
    @TRAN_TYPE_ID    = 12,
    @TRAN_DATE = '2 Jan 2024',
    @REF_ID       = 'DD-1',
    @AMOUNT     = 1600.00
```

2. Interest earned. Banking module.
```
exec sp_Process_Trans
    @TRAN_TYPE_ID    = 23,
    @TRAN_DATE = '6 Jan 2024',
    @REF_ID       = '1031',
    @AMOUNT     = 51.22
```

3. Utility bill payment. Accounts Payable and Expenses module.

    ```
    exec sp_Process_Trans
        @TRAN_TYPE_ID   = 11,
        @TRAN_DATE = '8 Jan 2024',
        @REF_ID     = '1097',
        @AMOUNT     = 103.00
    ```

4. Utility bill payment. Accounts Payable and Expenses module.

    ```
    exec sp_Process_Trans
        @TRAN_TYPE_ID   = 11,
        @TRAN_DATE = '9 Jan 2024',
        @REF_ID     = '617P',
        @AMOUNT     = 166.50
    ```

5. Travel / Fuel payment. Accounts Payable and Expenses module.

    ```
    exec sp_Process_Trans
        @TRAN_TYPE_ID   = 13,
        @TRAN_DATE = '10 Jan 2024',
        @REF_ID     = '3358 ',
        @AMOUNT     = 53.00
    ```

6. Client cash receipt. Accounts Receivable module.

    ```
    exec sp_Process_Trans
        @TRAN_TYPE_ID   = 16,
        @TRAN_DATE = '10 Jan 2024',
        @REF_ID     = '523',
        @AMOUNT     = 14500.00
    ```

7. Customer invoice. Accounts Receivable module.

    ```
    exec sp_Process_Trans
        @TRAN_TYPE_ID   = 15,
        @TRAN_DATE = '11 Jan 2024',
        @REF_ID     = '781',
        @AMOUNT     = 18500.00
    ```

8. Mortgage loan payment. Business Finance module.

    ```
    exec sp_Process_Trans
        @TRAN_TYPE_ID   = 6,
        @TRAN_DATE  = '16 Jan 2024',
        @REF_ID     = 'MP-5',
        @AMOUNT     = 1565.00,
        @INTEREST   = 462.75,
        @PRINCIPAL  = 1102.25
    ```

9. Monthly payroll. Payroll Module.

    ```
    exec sp_Process_Trans
        @TRAN_TYPE_ID   = 17,
        @TRAN_DATE  = '23 Jan 2024',
        @REF_ID     = '01/25',
        @AMOUNT     = 12500.00,
        @INCOME_TAX = 4500.00,
        @NET_PAY    = 8000.00
    ```

10. Net salary payment. Payroll module.

    ```
    exec sp_Process_Trans
        @TRAN_TYPE_ID   = 19,
        @TRAN_DATE  = '24 Jan 2024',
        @REF_ID     = '01/25',
        @AMOUNT     = 8000.00
    ```

11. Income tax payment. Payroll module.

    ```
    exec sp_Process_Trans
        @TRAN_TYPE_ID   = 18,
        @TRAN_DATE  = '24 Jan 2024',
        @REF_ID     = '01/25',
        @AMOUNT     = 4500.00
    ```

12. Client cash receipt. Accounts Receivable module.

    ```
    exec sp_Process_Trans
        @TRAN_TYPE_ID   = 16,
        @TRAN_DATE = '27 Jan 2024',
        @REF_ID     = '524',
        @AMOUNT     = 8500.00
    ```

13. Utility bill. Accounts Payable and Expenses module.
```
exec sp_Process_Trans
    @TRAN_TYPE_ID    = 10,
    @TRAN_DATE = '28 Jan 2024',
    @REF_ID        = '1098',
    @AMOUNT      = 103.00
```

14. Utility bill. Accounts Payable and Expenses module.
```
exec sp_Process_Trans
    @TRAN_TYPE_ID    = 10,
    @TRAN_DATE = '30 Jan 2024',
    @REF_ID        = '619',
    @AMOUNT      = 166.50
```

15. Long-term loan payment. Business Financing module.
```
exec sp_Process_Trans
    @TRAN_TYPE_ID    = 4,
    @TRAN_DATE = '31 Jan 2024',
    @REF_ID        = 'LTP-10',
    @AMOUNT      = 577.77,
    @INTEREST    = 77.77,
    @PRINCIPAL   = 500.00
```

16. Bank charges payment. Banking module.
```
exec sp_Process_Trans
    @TRAN_TYPE_ID    = 22,
    @TRAN_DATE = '31 Jan 2024',
    @REF_ID        = 'BC-9',
    @AMOUNT      = 12.50
```

February 2024 answers

1. Office rent payment. Accounts Payable and Expenses module.
```
exec sp_Process_Trans
    @TRAN_TYPE_ID    = 12,
    @TRAN_DATE= '2 Feb 2024',
    @REF_ID        = 'DD-2',
    @AMOUNT      = 1600.00
```

2. Interest earned. Banking module.
```
exec sp_Process_Trans
    @TRAN_TYPE_ID    = 23,
    @TRAN_DATE= '6 Feb 2024',
    @REF_ID        = '1032',
    @AMOUNT      = 51.22
```

3. Utility bill payment. Accounts Payable and Expenses module.
```
exec sp_Process_Trans
    @TRAN_TYPE_ID    = 11,
    @TRAN_DATE= '8 Feb 2024',
    @REF_ID        = '1098',
    @AMOUNT      = 103.00
```

4. Utility bill payment. Accounts Payable and Expenses module.
```
exec sp_Process_Trans
    @TRAN_TYPE_ID    = 11,
    @TRAN_DATE= '9 Feb 2024',
    @REF_ID        = '618P',
    @AMOUNT      = 166.50
```

5. Travel / Fuel payment. Accounts Payable and Expenses module.
```
exec sp_Process_Trans
    @TRAN_TYPE_ID    = 13,
    @TRAN_DATE= '10 Feb 2024',
    @REF_ID        = '3359 ',
    @AMOUNT      = 120.00
```

6. Client cash receipt. Accounts Receivable module.
```
exec sp_Process_Trans
    @TRAN_TYPE_ID    = 16,
    @TRAN_DATE= '10 Feb 2024',
    @REF_ID        = '524',
    @AMOUNT      = 15500.00
```

7. Customer invoice. Accounts Receivable module.

```
exec sp_Process_Trans
    @TRAN_TYPE_ID      = 15,
    @TRAN_DATE = '11 Feb 2024',
    @REF_ID        = '782',
    @AMOUNT     = 18500.00
```

8. Mortgage loan payment. Business Finance module.

```
exec sp_Process_Trans
    @TRAN_TYPE_ID      = 6,
    @TRAN_DATE = '16 Feb 2024',
    @REF_ID        = 'MP-6',
    @AMOUNT     = 1565.00,
    @INTEREST   = 462.75,
    @PRINCIPAL  = 1102.25
```

9. Monthly payroll. Payroll Module.

```
exec sp_Process_Trans
    @TRAN_TYPE_ID      = 17,
    @TRAN_DATE = '23 Feb 2024',
    @REF_ID        = '02/25',
    @AMOUNT     = 12500.00,
    @INCOME_TAX = 4500.00,
    @NET_PAY    = 8000.00
```

10. Net salary payment. Payroll module.

```
exec sp_Process_Trans
    @TRAN_TYPE_ID      = 19,
    @TRAN_DATE = '24 Feb 2024',
    @REF_ID        = '02/25',
    @AMOUNT     = 8000.00
```

11. Income tax payment. Payroll module.

```
exec sp_Process_Trans
    @TRAN_TYPE_ID      = 18,
    @TRAN_DATE = '24 Feb 2024',
    @REF_ID        = '02/25',
    @AMOUNT     = 4500.00
```

12. Client cash receipt. Accounts Receivable module.

```
exec sp_Process_Trans
    @TRAN_TYPE_ID      = 16,
    @TRAN_DATE = '26 Feb 2024',
    @REF_ID        = '525',
    @AMOUNT     = 10500.00
```

13. Utility bill. Accounts Payable and Expenses module.

```
exec sp_Process_Trans
    @TRAN_TYPE_ID      = 10,
    @TRAN_DATE = '27 Feb 2024',
    @REF_ID        = '1099',
    @AMOUNT     = 103.00
```

14. Utility bill. Accounts Payable and Expenses module.

```
exec sp_Process_Trans
    @TRAN_TYPE_ID      = 10,
    @TRAN_DATE = '27 Feb 2024',
    @REF_ID        = '620',
    @AMOUNT     = 166.50
```

15. Long-term loan payment. Business Financing module.

```
exec sp_Process_Trans
    @TRAN_TYPE_ID      = 4,
    @TRAN_DATE = '28 Feb 2024',
    @REF_ID        = 'LTP-11',
    @AMOUNT     = 577.77,
    @INTEREST   = 77.77,
    @PRINCIPAL  = 500.00
```

16. Bank charges payment. Banking module.

```
exec sp_Process_Trans
    @TRAN_TYPE_ID      = 22,
    @TRAN_DATE = '28 Feb 2024',
    @REF_ID        = 'BC-10',
    @AMOUNT     = 12.50
```

March 2024 answers

1. Office rent payment. Accounts Payable and Expenses module.

   ```
   exec sp_Process_Trans
       @TRAN_TYPE_ID    = 12,
       @TRAN_DATE = '2 Mar 2024',
       @REF_ID        = 'DD-3',
       @AMOUNT      = 1600.00
   ```

2. Interest earned. Banking module.

   ```
   exec sp_Process_Trans
       @TRAN_TYPE_ID    = 23,
       @TRAN_DATE = '6 Mar 2024',
       @REF_ID        = '1033',
       @AMOUNT      = 51.22
   ```

3. Utility bill payment. Accounts Payable and Expenses module.

   ```
   exec sp_Process_Trans
       @TRAN_TYPE_ID    = 11,
       @TRAN_DATE = '8 Mar 2024',
       @REF_ID        = '1099',
       @AMOUNT      = 103.00
   ```

4. Utility bill payment. Accounts Payable and Expenses module

   ```
   exec sp_Process_Trans
       @TRAN_TYPE_ID    = 11,
       @TRAN_DATE = '9 Mar 2024',
       @REF_ID        = '619P',
       @AMOUNT      = 166.50
   ```

5. Travel / Fuel payment. Accounts Payable and Expenses module.

   ```
   exec sp_Process_Trans
       @TRAN_TYPE_ID    = 13,
       @TRAN_DATE = '10 Mar 2024',
       @REF_ID        = '3360',
       @AMOUNT      = 35.50
   ```

6. Client cash receipt. Accounts Receivable module.

   ```
   exec sp_Process_Trans
       @TRAN_TYPE_ID    = 16,
       @TRAN_DATE = '10 Mar 2024',
       @REF_ID        = '525',
       @AMOUNT      = 12200.00
   ```

7. Customer invoice. Accounts Receivable module.

   ```
   exec sp_Process_Trans
       @TRAN_TYPE_ID    = 15,
       @TRAN_DATE = '12 Mar 2024',
       @REF_ID        = '783',
       @AMOUNT      = 21750.00
   ```

8. Customer invoice. Accounts Receivable module.

   ```
   exec sp_Process_Trans
       @TRAN_TYPE_ID    = 15,
       @TRAN_DATE = '13 Mar 2024',
       @REF_ID        = '784',
       @AMOUNT      = 11500.00
   ```

9. Mortgage loan payment. Business Finance module.

   ```
   exec sp_Process_Trans
       @TRAN_TYPE_ID    = 6,
       @TRAN_DATE  = '16 Mar 2024',
       @REF_ID        = 'MP-8',
       @AMOUNT      = 1565.00,
       @INTEREST    = 462.75,
       @PRINCIPAL  = 1102.25
   ```

10. Monthly payroll. Payroll Module.

    ```
    exec sp_Process_Trans
        @TRAN_TYPE_ID    = 17,
        @TRAN_DATE  = '23 Mar 2024',
        @REF_ID        = '03/25',
        @AMOUNT      = 12500.00,
        @INCOME_TAX        =
    4500.00,
        @NET_PAY      = 8000.00
    ```

11. Net salary payment. Payroll module.

```
exec sp_Process_Trans
    @TRAN_TYPE_ID    = 19,
    @TRAN_DATE = '24 Mar 2024',
    @REF_ID        = '03/25',
    @AMOUNT     = 8000.00
```

12. Income tax payment. Payroll module.

```
exec sp_Process_Trans
    @TRAN_TYPE_ID    = 18,
    @TRAN_DATE = '24 Mar 2024',
    @REF_ID        = '03/25',
    @AMOUNT     = 4500.00
```

13. Client cash receipt. Accounts Receivable module.

```
exec sp_Process_Trans
    @TRAN_TYPE_ID    = 16,
    @TRAN_DATE = '26 Mar 2024',
    @REF_ID        = '526',
    @AMOUNT     = 11250.00
```

14. Utility bill. Accounts Payable and Expenses module.

```
exec sp_Process_Trans
    @TRAN_TYPE_ID     = 10,
    @TRAN_DATE = '27 Mar 2024',
    @REF_ID        = '1100',
    @AMOUNT     = 103.00
```

15. Utility bill. Accounts Payable and Expenses module.

```
exec sp_Process_Trans
    @TRAN_TYPE_ID     = 10,
    @TRAN_DATE = '27 Mar 2024',
    @REF_ID        = '621',
    @AMOUNT     = 166.50
```

16. Long-term loan payment. Business Financing module.

```
exec sp_Process_Trans
    @TRAN_TYPE_ID     = 4,
    @TRAN_DATE = '30 Mar 2024',
    @REF_ID        = 'LTP-12',
    @AMOUNT     = 577.77,
    @INTEREST   = 77.77,
    @PRINCIPAL  = 500.00
```

17. Bank charges payment. Banking module.

```
exec sp_Process_Trans
    @TRAN_TYPE_ID     = 22,
    @TRAN_DATE = '31 Mar 2024',
    @REF_ID        = 'BC-11',
    @AMOUNT     = 12.50
```

18. Owner cash withdrawal. Business Financing module.

```
exec sp_Process_Trans
    @TRAN_TYPE_ID     = 2,
    @TRAN_DATE = '31 Mar 2024',
    @REF_ID        = 'CW-2',
    @AMOUNT     = 3500.00
```

Index

Acknowledgments

I extend my gratitude to the brilliant colleagues I have worked with over the years. This book is the result of collective wisdom built through collaboration. Sharpening one another, like iron, provided the perfect continuous learning experience for all of us.

Many thanks to TJ (Tom Jackson) for his technical scrutiny and invaluable feedback. My deep appreciation to the beta readers Kam Bawa, Emma Forest, and George Peltier for the quality and thoroughness of their reviews.

And much gratitude to my best friend, Tembi, for always being there, and to Ruvheneko, for his cover design input and continuous cheerleading.

ABOUT THE AUTHOR

Chris Chinaire has worked in every role
in IT Systems Development Projects
over the last three decades.
He has been involved in the development,
customisation, support and implementation
of financial modules,
gaining a strong understanding of
accounting principles from a technical perspective.
His experience spans the
finance, healthcare, and legal sectors.
He is based in South London, England,
where he works as a Data Management
and Business Intelligence consultant.
His professional memberships
include TDWI and IIBA.